COPING SUCCESSFULLY WITH RSI

MAGGIE BLACK is a writer and journalist, specializing in international social issues. She has written on many health-related topics, including HIV/AIDS, maternal and child health, and water and environmental sanitation. Her books include *Children First: the story of UNICEF* (OUP, 1996). She has survived computer-induced RSI since 1992, and attended the pain management inpatient clinic, INPUT, at St Thomas' Hospital. In this book she draws on these experiences, advocating the kind of approaches she has found successful.

PENNY GRAY is a freelance medical writer, with a PhD in psychopharmacology and a career that includes heading a team of writing staff at a top European medical education agency. Her many years' experience in medical writing ranges from highly technical publications, to more popular materials for GPs and other healthcare workers and the general public. Her output includes books and articles on almost every aspect of medicine and health.

'Listen when your body tries to tell you something is wrong. Pain is a warning signal. Your body whispers to you. If you ignore the whispers, it talks. If you ignore the talking, it shouts. Eventually it will go on strike and refuse to work at all.'

Bunny Martin, Director, Body Action Campaign

Overcoming Common Problems

Coping Successfully with RSI

An essential guide for computer users

Maggie Black and Penny Gray

First published in Great Britain in 1999 by
Sheldon Press, SPCK, Marylebone Road, London NW1 4DU

British Library Cataloguing-in-Publication Data
A catalogue record for this book is available from the British Library

ISBN 0–85969–811–4

Typeset by Deltatype Limited, Birkenhead, Merseyside
Printed in Great Britain by
Biddles Ltd, Guildford and King's Lynn

Contents

Acknowledgements

A number of people have helped in the preparation of this book, in particular Dr Charles Pither and the team at the INPUT Pain Management Programme at St Thomas' Hospital, who encouraged the project from the start. Among others who offered useful information and advice, and/or reviewed sections of the manuscript, are the following: Jenny Baker, Katrina Billings, Professor Howard Bird, Vreni Booth, Ray Broome, Ann Bruce, Wendy Chalmers-Mill, Chris Chapman, Kelston Chorley, Mary Crowther-Alwyn, Lynne Davies, Natalie Davenport, Janet Duchesne, Bill Fine, Dr Chris Glynn, Jane Greening, Sissel Fowler, Vicki Harding, Dr Richard Harrington, Dr Edward Huskisson, Dr Michael Hutson, Irmela Jay, Graham Jukes, Julie Kelly, Wendy Lawrence, Karen Mejlaender, Bunny Martin, Ted Oakes, Nicola Plested, Gretel Quick, Louanne Richards, Gideon Reeve, David Robinson, Craig Simmons, Sharyn Singer, Andy Tippett, Owen Tudor, Paul Wolf. We would also like to thank all those RSI survivors who sent us their stories or agreed to be interviewed for the book. Many have been quoted in the text. Others' contributions helped inform our understanding of what it is to experience – and cope with – RSI, even if their own words do not appear.

Maggie Black and Penny Gray

Foreword

In 1864 Samuel Solly published an article in the Lancet, based on a lecture he delivered at St Thomas' Hospital on 'Scrivener's Palsy'. In his lecture he described the sad fate of individuals afflicted with this troublesome condition. His account includes a number of case histories with many of the sufferers giving first-hand reports of their difficulties. Readers of this book would find these depressingly familiar.

Patients describe how their problems start with pain in the hand which they initially think must be a sprain, although they cannot recall an injury. They take a break from their writing tasks and – sure enough – the pain settles down. Unfortunately the pain returns on recommencing work, and seems to spread. They do not feel that they are suffering from a serious complaint and are relaxed about the likely cause, not thinking it to be of any great consequence.

When the symptoms persist a little longer they consult a doctor who suggests various diagnoses, including rheumatism. The doctor makes some recommendations but these seem to be of little benefit. The sufferer returns to work only to find that the pain becomes worse and spreads up the arm. The symptoms persist and it becomes increasingly difficult to carry on. Then they start becoming anxious and worried.

What if the condition does not get better?

Could it possibly be something serious?

What treatment do they need?

Do they need to see another doctor?

Perhaps they take a further break from work and find, once again, that the symptoms settle down. However, on returning to work the intensity of the pain is magnified and extends into the whole arm, and maybe into the neck. Alas, very often they reach the situation where they have to stop work again. However, on this occasion they find, alarmingly, that the pain does not go when they cease work. They return to their doctor, who is becoming increasingly exasperated. The doctor's simple suggestions and treatments have failed, so they come up with stranger explanations as to the cause of the pain, and offer more outrageous remedies. All too often the unhappy scenario ends in the individual losing their job and being unable to work, now with a seemingly permanent disability.

To those familiar with the modern-day affliction best known as RSI, the question could well be asked: So what has changed in the last 135 years?

Medical science, with its glittering array of technological and pharmaco-logical treatments and cures, appears to have made little progress with the problem of upper limb pain.

If anything, the situation is worse. Sedentary lifestyles and occupations have increased the number of sufferers, and the condition is now closely associated with use of the computer, a piece of equipment found in every office and many people's homes. This has led to media interest and public curiosity over this mysterious condition. All the stakeholders, upon whom the consequences of upper limb pain impinge, have an opinion about its aetiology, treatment, and the reality of the pain experience.

The traditional medical scientific view is that nothing abnormal can be detected, and therefore the condition is not based in tissue pathology. The legal system opines that the illness is related to seeking compensation or medical retirement. Employers think that it is about failure to cope and work-shyness. Psychiatrists, often called in to give a view of the individual's mental status, usually find no evidence of mental illness but have little constructive information to offer. As a result of the diversity of opinions, sensible advice and effective treatment are elusive. The sufferer is either left on their own, or reduced to seeking out support and advice from other sufferers, which can be emotionally charged. The view that all is hopeless and nothing can be done remains prominent and unchallenged. Is this really the case?

No! All is not quite as it seems. Looking a little further, seeing between the entrenched attitudes and the dogma, there is a group of sufferers who have got better from RSI. They have had effective treatment, developed strategies both physical and psychological to cope with their problems, and returned to fulfilling and enjoyable lives. They have often returned to work in a remunerative and fulfilling occupation.

How have they done it?

They have done it for themselves. Instead of seeing themselves as hapless victims of a devastating disease process, they have come to terms with the various factors that led to their difficulties, adopted a positive approach, and using a number of different techniques have learnt to take control of their symptoms and manage their pain. Inevitably, this is a more difficult option than the magic cure. The problem is that the magic cure is no more available in 1999 than it was for Samuel Solly all those years ago.

The reason is that there is no single lesion to account for the disparate and complex difficulties experienced with this condition. RSI, like a number of other poorly understood medical conditions, is truly a 'whole person' problem. To understand it even partially, one needs to understand links between mind, body and environment that we know to be relevant in other settings, but often choose to ignore when it comes to our own illness.

Treatment in the form of pain management can be effective for the person who wants to make it work. All too often, this approach is delayed by years of fruitless searching and ineffective therapy. How different things could be if this integrated, 'whole person' approach was utilized at the outset, rather than as the last resort when all else has failed.

In this book, Maggie Black and Penny Gray document the experiences of upper limb pain sufferers based on first-hand evidence. They then set out a rational series of steps involving a number of techniques, which if pursued assiduously will undoubtedly result in improvements in function and well-being. This approach to pain management, and the techniques they describe, are in many cases based upon the techniques we have been imparting here at INPUT to RSI and other chronic pain sufferers in our residential pain management courses.

This approach and the techniques it deploys may seem like a tough option. But the unpalatable reality is that they are the only option. The most difficult step is the first: deciding that this is what I must do in order to get better. Those who wait for the miraculous saviour to deliver them back to perfect health are, unfortunately, destined to wait an awfully long time.

Charles Pither
Medical Director
INPUT Pain Management Programme
St Thomas' Hospital, London

Authors' Note

The term 'repetitive strain injury', and its abbreviation, RSI, are usually used by sufferers of computer-induced pain and other overuse syndromes to refer to their condition, though these are not terms normally used by the medical profession.

Throughout this book, we use the medically imprecise but popular term, 'RSI', to describe pain in the hands, wrists, arms and upper body associated with computer use and other types of employment or occupation that demand repetitive action, for example, assembly-line work or playing a musical instrument. The major symptom in most cases is severe and persistent pain in the hands and arms; there can also be tingling, numbness and cramping in the neck, shoulders and back. In many people the symptoms are diffuse and do not usually respond well to either conventional or alternative treatments. How to manage diffuse RSI is the main subject of this book.

We have aimed the book primarily at computer users. However, the approach outlined is applicable to anyone with any RSI condition, at any stage of development, whatever the cause. With RSI, as with any condition of ill health, prevention is far better than cure. The management regime proposed in this book is equally applicable for those who simply feel they are at risk; those who already have some preliminary RSI symptoms; and those who have actually developed this debilitating and mysterious condition.

Maggie Black
Penny Gray PhD

1

What on earth is my computer doing to me?

The onset of computer pain

To begin with there are just a few aches and pains, probably in your right arm. It is difficult to say where they are exactly, to pinpoint an actual location. Sometimes the hand or wrist hurts. Occasionally a finger gives a tiny shriek of dismay. For many people, the upper arm seems to be the most frequent and loudest complainer – for others, the shoulder or neck.

These are warning signs. The body has a method – pain – to tell us that something is wrong. But many computer users ignore it. There is pressure at work, deadlines in a busy office. The article must be written, the data must be entered, the brief is needed by tomorrow.

The muscles start up their low decibel protest when you have been sitting at the computer for several hours. Or maybe it's only after you stop. As weeks go by, the aching feeling comes on earlier. It crescendos to a throb. Faint pins and needles become sharper – hedgehogs seem to be invading your arm. When you stop work, the aching or tingling continues for a while. And gradually, for longer.

As the condition progresses, you start to take evasive action. When the pain comes on, you use the left hand on its own. But then that begins to play up, too. So the right arm is brought back into use. But its protest begins earlier every day. A machine which used to be your friend is now becoming distinctly hostile.

A holiday intervenes. Good, you say to yourself. A chance to stop work, rest your arms, no working on the computer for some weeks. A good, long break will put you back into the comfort zone and re-enlist your computer as your ally.

But it doesn't.

On the holiday, you have nagging doubts. Every now and again – carrying luggage, driving the car, holding up a book to read – there's a twinge. Just enough to remind you that your arm is fragile, prone to displays of temperament. Within a day or two of being back at your desk, it's grumbling solidly at you again. But you are still in denial. You plough on. You make little concessions to try to relieve the pressure. You don't correct typing errors. You see whether your left hand is able to use the mouse.

By now you are becoming alarmed. Your neck, back and shoulder seem to have become involved – is this 'computer disease' spreading? If weeks of no computer use didn't make any difference – and there is absolutely no doubt in your mind that the computer is the villain of the piece – what are you going to do? Maybe you go and see your GP. He or she may be sympathetic, but have little to propose beyond rest, painkillers and a bit of physio. Or decidedly unhelpful, and suggest that you are only suffering from stress and that the physical symptoms are 'nothing to worry about'.

In the meantime, your work begins to suffer. Half your mind is waiting for the pain, monitoring the pain, trying to ignore the pain. Your concentration weakens and your work makes its way onto the screen slowly and with increasing difficulty. The day's output shrinks. You begin to feel miserable and aggrieved.

By this time, the experience of the pain is also beginning to tire you. At the end of the day you slump in front of the television fit for nothing, or retire to bed. Pain that ebbs and flows but doesn't really go away is also depressing, even if it is not so severe that you can't sleep or carry out life's tasks more or less functionally. You start taking painkillers, but it doesn't respond consistently. And it is frightening. Will your arms and hands seize up altogether? Every few minutes, you find you are monitoring your body's discordant song. Is it louder, or softer? Please, you beseech it, *shut up.*

'I had been working hard all the academic year. So the house was filthy, and I scrubbed it for a week. My arms ached after that, but then we had a long holiday. I was fine. When I went back to work, I began to feel bad again. Then I spent one whole day moving heavy furniture. That evening I couldn't use my arms. I went from "bad" to "absolutely dreadful".' *Frances, university lecturer*

Your new preoccupation begins to dominate both your personal life and your working life. From being a minor irritant, the pain in your arms and upper body becomes a central feature of your existence. It feeds your anxiety, and your anxiety makes it worse.

If your livelihood depends on computer use, the hideous prospect looms that you won't be able to carry on. If you are in a job, you will have to discuss your debility with your employer, with goodness knows what result. So you put it off. If you are self-employed, you discuss it endlessly with yourself. But your personal resources – of energy, optimism, capacity to plan – are themselves reduced. Just keeping on day to day may become a struggle, with horizons closing in around you.

One day, your body shrieks 'Stop!'

'I had had some symptoms before, but I had a period of overworking badly. It happened very fast – suddenly, I lost the use of my hands. It felt like I was plugging my fingers into an electric socket.' *Richard, software developer.*

Maybe you wake up in the morning in excruciating pain and just know you can't go to work. Maybe while you are battling on, trying to complete an assignment, your whole upper body suddenly begins to feel inflamed. Or your hands shake uncontrollably. Or your body feels as if it has become infected with needle-sharp gremlins flooding into your nervous system. The keyboard lies there, innocent and supine. But you only have to look at it for your body to scream.

By now you have become a full-blown sufferer of computer-induced pain, what most people refer to as repetitive strain injury, or RSI. Temporarily at least, you have to abandon the demon keyboard altogether. You get a note from the doctor and go sick.

But what if you are self-employed, and that's not an option? Perhaps you decide to write by hand instead. And then you discover that the condition has become so entrenched that writing by hand is by now as painful as using a computer. What *can* you do?

Desperation descends. Does serious disability threaten? Are you going to have to throw away all your professional dreams and ambitions? What are you going to live on?

'I thought I'd write by hand instead. Then I found I couldn't write either. I remember walking along feeling quite numb, and wondering, "What will I do for the rest of my life?" ' *Rosemary, university researcher*

Are you a potential user of this book?

What has been described here is a path trodden by increasing numbers of people. It is a path also known to other kinds of workers who have nothing to do with the computer – those whose work requires constant repetition of small movements, or the use of precision tools or instruments while the body is in a state of tension. Musicians, assembly-line workers, dentists and many other types of workers are occupationally at risk. But it is the computer which has lifted RSI from

3

a minority phenomenon to a significant workplace-induced disease condition.

The growing use of computers in work and leisure lives means that ever more people are suffering from associated pain. Some experience only the early symptoms – the occasional ache or pain in hand, arm or wrist. But if action is not taken to change the relationship between the person's body and the use of his or her computer, the accumulating problems can eventually lead to serious debility – even disability.

The explosion of home computer use means that many young people spend their free time in front of a screen, playing games or surfing the net. They too are vulnerable. Their bodies may be willing to put up with computer-induced abuse now, but in later life they may pay – how severely we cannot yet know. They need encouragement to use their addictive machine in body-friendly ways.

Recent research by neurophysiologists suggests that most people who regularly use computers develop some degree of nerve damage in their arms. Perhaps this is an occupational hazard that computer users will have to accommodate. Monitoring the body's behaviour around the computer and taking timely action to control the damage is currently the only option – barring modifications to the computer system itself.

What factors influence why some people become more seriously affected than others? The amount of time they spend at the keyboard is obviously one. There are many others. The differences in people's physical fitness, occupation, work-station set-up, attitude to life, office environment and modes of computer use play as great a part in the severity of the condition as any characteristic of the computer itself.

'If you love your work, if you have an almost obsessive relationship with your work, as I do, that makes you vulnerable.' *Richard, software developer*

Individual differences are recognized in the approach adopted in this book towards preventing, managing and getting rid of RSI. It is primarily written with computer users in mind, but its recipe for dealing with RSI is applicable for any kind of sufferer. Its contents are designed in such a way that you can pick and choose what you think is most appropriate for you. *You* will be the person in the driving seat, taking control over your actual or prospective condition.

Perhaps you are one of those who have started to feel some negative effects from repetitive activity, but have managed to stow this information away in the back of your mind. 'I'll ease up if it gets worse,' you say, without realizing just how much worse it might suddenly get, and then how disabling it could be.

In your case, this book will equip you to make manageable changes in your relationship with your job, with the computer and work-station, and with yourself, which will prevent the condition from deteriorating.

If you are already suffering seriously from computer pain, this book can help you cope with your condition, hopefully master it and get your life back on track.

If you suffer from RSI, the entrenchment of the condition in your body will almost certainly have been accompanied by growing distress, fear and anxiety. You may have received unhelpful or unsympathetic advice from members of the medical profession. Your employer may have reacted poorly, hinting – or worse – that you have become a liability and should leave. You wonder how on earth you'll find another job or the money to retrain for another occupation.

> 'The attitude at work seems to be: "The company doctor has seen you, we've given you physiotherapy, we've done our bit." They've met their legal obligations and that's it.' *James, journalist*

You see your problem stretching away indefinitely into the future, with profound implications for your income, sense of self-worth and outlook on life. You may feel let down by friends in whom you confide because they don't understand how devastated you are. Unlike a broken leg, your condition won't mend in a prescribed period and they don't know what to say. You feel profoundly depressed and isolated.

All these aspects of the condition are addressed in this book in an integrated fashion with the pain itself.

But before you get started, you will almost certainly want an explanation of what is happening. You have probably asked yourself again and again: 'How can my computer cause this pain?' It doesn't bite. You can't lose your hand in its crunching machinery. So what on earth is going on?

The roots of the problem

Over the course of human history, human beings have gradually become less and less active. But the extraordinary combination of hard and soft tissues of which we are made wasn't designed to be inactive and shouldn't be misused in that way.

Our bodies evolved millions of years ago, and are constructed for the lifestyle of long-distant ancestors who lived physically strenuous lives. People who lived by hunting and gathering kept constantly on the move. Farming – the occupation of most people for most of the last two millennia – is an energetic and active occupation, especially when non-mechanized.

When more people began working in factories and offices after the industrial revolution, our lives became more sedentary and we became less fit. But the greatest drop in human activity levels has come in the past few decades, in the age of television and the computer. The majority of people sit for an average of 8–10 hours a day, at home, at work, when we're socializing or travelling by motorized transport. People have become seriously unfit. Our bodies are stiff. Our muscles are shrunken, weak and sluggish, our bones thinner and our joints inelastic.

Sitting for long stretches in the same position puts far more strain on the body than the strenuous physical activity its muscles, bones and joints were designed to perform.

If a person is unfit, the body's mechanisms are already functioning below par – stalled, creaking, reluctant.

Add to this slumped shoulders, an unsupported lower back, a bent neck, eyes fixed and head locked into one position, a poking-forward chin and generally poor posture.

Perhaps add a bad chair, too high or low a desk, a screen or keyboard at the wrong angle.

On top of this, add a mental state of intense concentration, psychological or emotional stress, and total lack of bodily self-awareness.

Then add a constantly repeated 'unnatural' action, undertaken at the extremities. It involves no large-scale movement and most of the body makes no contribution to it. The solid, still, tensed mass of the body is being repeatedly jarred at the edges by the equivalent of a small pneumatic drill.

Some combination of these factors means that the body's communication system has been thoroughly primed to become jangled and confused. As the drill goes on and on, intricate nervous pathways stop functioning properly. Danger signals are being transmitted, but in a muted or confusing sort of way. They are not picked up, perhaps because the person can't feel them properly. The body's system of shouting 'you are undergoing damage' seems to have gone awry.

It's not as if a sledgehammer dropped onto your hands, crushing them and producing injuries you can see. It's much more subtle and complicated. So the signals are overlooked. The mind continues to impose its will on the body and insist that arms and hands keep tapping away. The nervous pathways scramble, the muscles become sore, and the pain intensifies and turns up in new locations.

'I kept my right arm on the mouse, finger pointing, waiting for the next action, while my left hand did the keyboarding. I did not withdraw my right hand and put it in my lap. Keeping it rigid in one position – that's what did me in!' *Teresa, graphic designer*

So what is the medical explanation?

Repetitive strain disorders are by no means new. In fact, they were first described in 1713 by the father of occupational medicine, the Italian Professor Bernadino Ramazzini of Modena. He called them 'diseases of workers' and described how the 'incessant driving of pen over paper causes intense fatigue of the hand and the whole arm'. Nearly 300 years ago, he appreciated the involvement of the whole nervous system. Since that time, similar conditions have been experienced by people in various factory and agricultural occupations – hop pickers, fish gutters and biscuit packers, for example.

When computer pain conditions first began to surface widely in the mid-1980s, sufferers were initially greeted with scepticism. No diagnostic test, scan or X-ray provided evidence of physical illness. But the label 'repetitive strain injury' or RSI quickly emerged and began to be commonly used to describe the condition.

Industrial workers with repetitive pain conditions have usually found it very difficult to obtain recognition that they were suffering from an 'industrial disease'. The arrival of computer-induced pain syndromes made RSI a much better-known phenomenon and gave it more clout since it affected better-paid, highly trained professionals. However, journalists and office workers trying to convince employers and the courts that they were genuinely suffering from a disabling complaint – and medical specialists speaking on their behalf – were rebuffed, just like others before them.

The problem is that doctors don't entirely know, in scientific terms, what is going on. There is no conclusive proof for an underlying pathology. Most RSI experts would agree that the condition is complex and has multiple inter-related causes. Four factors in particular stand out: lots of *repetitive movements*; *sustained awkward or poor posture*; use of *excessive force* – hammering at the keyboard, for example; and *psychological stress*, perhaps due to work overload or punishing deadlines.

However, doctors are deeply divided about why some combination of these factors can translate into chronic pain in some people. Different theories abound. The most popular fall into three camps: *neurogenic* (nerve-related), *psychogenic* (mind-related), and *musculogenic* (muscle-related).

Neurogenic theories suggest that RSI consists of damage to the nerves, either locally, in the hands, arms and/or shoulders, or centrally, in the spinal cord. Compression of the nerves in many different places would explain why poor posture is an important factor – perhaps the most important – in the development of RSI. Likewise, involvement of the central nervous system would explain why people with symptoms in one hand develop symptoms in the other when they switch hands in an attempt to resolve the problem: nerve signals from both arms are centrally processed.

Until recently there was no evidence of nerve damage to back any neurogenic theory. But a few studies now claim to show sub-clinical changes in the nerves of RSI sufferers. The studies are small-scale and the findings need to be confirmed. If they turn out to be correct, they may provide the basis for quantitative assessment of diffuse RSI. This would be a breakthrough, especially for proving the condition in a court of law. So a lot rides on this – controversial – research.

Psychogenic theories of RSI suggest that it originates in the mind. Many of these theories are intensely patient-blaming. Some doctors assume that RSI sufferers imagine or exaggerate their symptoms in order to claim disability benefits and compensation. Others claim that RSI only affects personalities with anxious or obsessive tendencies. Yet others argue that RSI is psychosomatic – that the symptoms are directly caused by psychological stress. It's true that stress is certainly a contributory factor in most cases. However, there is little, if any, supporting evidence that it is a primary cause.

Musculogenic theories suggest that problems in the muscles are at the root of RSI. This would seem sensible given that many related conditions involve recognizable inflammation of muscles, tendons or other soft tissue. However, while these conditions – such as tenosynovitis and epicondylitis – are diagnosable from specific signs, obvious to the clinician, most cases of RSI are usually not, as described more fully in Chapter 2. In these cases of so-called diffuse RSI, proposed inflammation and build-up of toxins in the tissues have not been scientifically proved.

The true explanation is likely to involve some combination of mechanical and psychological factors. At present, because no pathology exists, many doctors fall back on psychogenic or 'in-the-mind' theories. Certainly there is an emotional component to pain. But the fact that conventional diagnosis has not yet confirmed a pathology doesn't mean that none exists. And many questions remain. For example, what makes some people more susceptible to RSI than others? In a study of factory workers, only 2 per cent of those doing exactly the same repetitive task developed RSI. This may reflect differences in postural habits, neuromuscular function, reactions to stress, or a genetic predisposition to the disorder. The jury is still out on this one, too.

What do I call my condition?

RSI is not a formally recognized medical condition. It is a description rather than a diagnosis. And the subject of much controversy among medical specialists. The 'I' for injury is particularly controversial because no conventional injury in medical terms – acute trauma-related tissue damage – can be discerned. And in the view of most medical experts, if no 'injury' is discernible, the condition shouldn't technically be called one. Indeed, whether using a computer can cause injury or not has been hotly contested in the courts.

So medical specialists in general avoid the term RSI. Instead, they have come up with a plethora of labels – 165 different disease codes were recorded in 1995, according to the US National Institute for Occupational Safety and Health. Among these, 'cumulative trauma disorder' is favoured in the US; 'occupational overuse syndrome' in New Zealand; 'cervicobrachial disorder' in Japan; and 'upper limb disorder' or 'work-related upper limb disorder' in the UK.

Most of these terms are vague and unsatisfactory for sufferers. The lack of a neat, and sufficiently compelling, name for their problem seems to relegate it to the nuisance level of something minor, trivial and boring. So they tend to use the term RSI simply because it has recognition value – people have come to know what it means, and are able to acknowledge that the condition is serious.

Sufferers desperately want people – family, friends, medical consultants, employers – to take their problem seriously. But they are thwarted by the fact that most RSIs are non-specific. The way that they are hidden in the body is one of their most daunting and mystifying characteristics.

In fact, it is this aspect of RSI which, more than any other, makes it so difficult to deal with. The modern medical approach to disease consists of diagnostic testing, followed by pharmaceutical or surgical intervention. In layman's terms, 'identify the problem, and provide a medical solution'. But most RSI is horribly elusive.

So what can doctors do for you? This is the next chapter.

2

There must be some medical solution

Getting a diagnosis

If you're experiencing worrying RSI-like symptoms your first port of call will probably be your GP. And your first question is likely to be: 'What is wrong with me? Why am I in such pain?' Diagnosis of your condition is important because the chosen method of treatment or management depends on the answer to this question.

If you are a long-time RSI sufferer, you may have already embarked on a medical merry-go-round, trawling from GP to physiotherapist, from specialist consultant to pain clinic. For the reasons explained in the previous chapter, you have very likely been given a bewildering range of views – some opposing – on your condition.

How to make sense of it all can become a secondary preoccupation, alongside the major one concerning the pain and how to get rid of it. Not being able to get a clear answer to this diagnosis question is normal. You are not alone! No-one understands the condition fully.

Whatever happens when you go to your GP, don't let your symptoms be dismissed. If you know that your symptoms are related to using a computer or some other kind of equipment, don't give way in the face of scepticism. Today, fewer GPs than was the case a few years ago will be unhelpful and dismissive, but some still exist and you may be unlucky. You may be greeted by: 'That's not RSI, that's just a sore hand.' That might be true in the early stages, but it suggests no ameliorative strategy. Preventing RSI is far, far better and easier than trying to cure it once it has set in. If you feel you're not being taken seriously, ask to see someone else.

'My GP never took my RSI seriously. On one visit he told me it was just my age. On another, he said, "You're unemployed, you've got too much time to sit around thinking about your aches and pains." And when I was working again, he put it down to stress!' *Teresa, graphic designer*

Even if your GP is sympathetic, he or she is unlikely to be able to help you much directly. Perhaps splints will be discussed, and rest, and maybe the use of hot and cold packs. GPs who have had direct

11

experience of RSI, or are very enlightened, may be able to offer something more. But undoubtedly the most valuable thing your GP can do is recognize the condition and its potential seriousness in your life, since the GP is not only the first line of medical defence against the condition, but the arbiter to the rest of the world over whether you are suffering from something serious or not.

The GP can also refer you on to a physiotherapist, or to medical specialists who may be able to offer diagnosis and treatment that the GP cannot. However, waiting lists for NHS physiotherapy clinics and consultant specialists may mean that many weeks pass before you get an appointment. If you are in a state of crisis, this presents another problem.

'I couldn't get an appointment with my GP for several days. So I went through the *Yellow Pages* and contacted a physiotherapist. This physio was a great help. When I did see the GP, he gave me anti-inflammatories, and referred me to an NHS physio. The waiting list was four to six weeks.' *Jim, software technician*

Doctor, please get rid of the pain

One of the most important things to understand about established RSI is that it is a *chronic pain* condition, not an *acute pain* condition – there is a vital difference. Chronic pain is pain that has persisted for more than six months – in spite of all attempts to relieve it. If you have been experiencing pain for several weeks, you may well have preliminary symptoms of RSI which have not yet become chronic. So the following information still applies.

Acute pain has a function: it acts as a warning signal to the body of new damage. It may last a few seconds, hours or days, even weeks, but it stops eventually – when the injury that caused it has healed.

Chronic pain appears to have no function. It does not indicate new damage; indeed, its cause is obscure. Many people with chronic pain have had an injury at some stage, and the pain has persisted, even though the actual injury has long since healed. The reasons are not understood, but are thought to be somehow related to changes in the nerves; something seems to have gone wrong with the way they behave which causes the pain signals to persist long after they should logically have ceased.

Thus, instead of doing something helpful to the body as does acute pain, chronic pain debilitates. In contrast to acute pain, chronic pain is emotionally and physically destructive.

'A person shouldn't be getting aches and pains from their work. Anything that doesn't settle overnight and builds up during the working week is a chronic condition. The problem with RSI is that it generally builds up slowly over months.' *Julie, physiotherapist*

Painkilling drugs

When a person suffers from pain, the one piece of medical technology easily available – across the counter or from the GP – is pain medication. This mainly takes the form of pills; there are also some gels and creams with painkilling ingredients.

Analgesics are the first-line treatment for most types of pain. They include the non-steroidal anti-inflammatory drugs (NSAIDs), such as aspirin and ibuprofen; paracetamol; and opioids such as codeine. All of these can be purchased in various strengths without a prescription. Many NSAIDs are available as creams or gels as well as pills. Some painkilling drugs (co-codamol, for example) combine two or more types of ingredient.

The stronger opioids, such as morphine and pethidine, are only available on prescription and are normally reserved for treating post-operative pain and cancer pain because of their severe side-effects on the central nervous system.

Anti-inflammatories act on inflamed nerve endings, to reduce pain and swelling. They are wonderful for treating acute pain, as in toothache or a broken ankle. But, like the other standard painkilling drugs, they are not designed for treating chronic pain. Painkillers may take the edge off chronic pain, but the effect is usually slight and short-lived – maybe an hour or so. Often they have little effect, and people end up using them more as a psychological crutch than for physical reasons.

Long-term, regular use of painkilling drugs can have other negative effects. Over time, NSAIDs tend to irritate the stomach lining, and can cause gastric ulcers. They also affect kidney function. And if they do help, they can encourage you to overstrain your body, causing further pain in the long run.

Other tablets that may be prescribed for RSI include antidepressants and tranquillizers. Low doses of so-called tricyclic antidepressants, such as amitriptyline, are thought to have some specific painkilling

13

effect in chronic pain conditions such as RSI. Low doses of antidepressants are also sometimes prescribed as hypnotics (i.e. sleeping tablets), while at higher doses they are used to lift low mood, a common consequence of chronic pain. However, all antidepressants have unwanted side-effects: daytime drowsiness, impairment of concentration and judgement, dry mouth, giddiness and difficulty passing water are some of the more common ones.

Tranquillizers can help you sleep and calm you down, and may sometimes help to reduce muscle spasm. However, they can also slow you to such an extent that you feel tired and more depressed. Moreover, the body becomes tolerant to them within a matter of days or weeks, so they become less effective and potentially habit-forming. Thus they are generally recommended for short-term use (two to four weeks) only. If you take tranquillizers for a longer period, your body becomes habituated to them, and withdrawal results in a number of unpleasant effects, including rebound anxiety and insomnia – the symptoms that probably led you to take them in the first place.

All types of painkillers should be avoided for long-term use in treatment of RSI. They may help at the height of a crisis or a flare-up, while you get a long-term management strategy in place. But that should be the limit of their use. If you start to see tablets as the only way to relieve pain – however ineffective – this can stop you looking for other, more adaptive ways of coping, as described in this book. And who knows what toxic effects all these tablets may have on your body when taken long term?

Other first-line medical treatments

Besides painkilling drugs, your GP may recommend use of a wrist splint for postural correction, or hot and cold packs to reduce symptoms in the forearm, hand or wrist. Both can be purchased inexpensively at pharmacy chainstores or, in the case of hot and cold compresses, also at sports shops. Cold packs can certainly give good, though temporary, relief of symptoms. If you don't want to go to the expense of buying a custom-made pack, you can improvise with a wine cooler or bag of frozen peas. Make sure you put a cloth between yourself and the freezer pack, to prevent its sticking to the skin.

Wrist splints are for immobilizing the wrist joint in a neutral position, particularly during sleep. Use them with care! Overuse of wrist splints can increase pain in the long term, and may cause muscle wasting, both of which can prevent or delay return of full limb function. And people who use them long term can become very psychologically dependent on them – a big hindrance to recovery. Wrist splints should never be used while you are working as this can exacerbate the problem. Immobility is likely to have contributed to the condition in the first place, and restoring and maintaining joint and muscle movement is part of the remedy.

The principal medical treatment: physiotherapy

The most likely referral your GP will make is to a physiotherapist. If he or she does not propose this, *ask for it*! And try to make sure that the physio to whom you are being referred has been trained specifically to treat RSI. Some physios – including NHS – are now highly trained in RSI treatment and have a lot of experience with RSI patients. Seeing a physio who is appropriately trained and seeing one who is not is the difference between night and day. If your GP is really unhelpful, consider going privately to a recommended RSI-trained physio.

'My physio gave me some stretching exercises for my hands and fingers. But all the muscles across my shoulders, neck and upper back are like steel. The physio keeps saying, "I think this", "I think that." I want someone who knows.' *Teresa, graphic designer*

Pain relief: electrotherapy

Physiotherapists may employ a number of special methods of pain relief. Electrotherapy covers any treatment based on the application of electromagnetic or ultrasonic energy, and includes ultrasound – one of the more common – interferential electrotherapy, pulsed short-wave diathermy and laser treatment. The use of ultrasound and laser beams focused on a painful point is of limited benefit for the diffuse types of pain experienced by most RSI sufferers. Indeed, the value of all such treatments for RSI is doubtful.

Transcutaneous electrical nerve stimulation (TENS) is an electrotherapy often used for treatment of painful conditions, and may provide some relief from the pain of RSI. TENS delivers small electrical impulses through electrode pads attached to your skin at painful points. The impulses stimulate nerves that carry touch sensations, closing a gating mechanism in the spinal cord to pain signals from the same site.

TENS machines are small, battery-powered and portable, and thus more convenient than other forms of electrotherapy. The physiotherapist may loan you a machine for home use, or they can be purchased at some pharmaceutical chainstores. If you buy one yourself, get a trained person, ideally a physiotherapist, to show you how to use it, and persist with it for at least a month under supervision. However, most people find that even if TENS helps to begin with, it becomes less effective as time goes on. Thus it is best used as part of a pain management strategy, as outlined later in this book.

'My problem is exacerbated by stress at work. A holiday helped to settle it down and a TENS machine was recommended by the physio. I bought one and, inconvenience aside, it is undoubtedly beneficial, and has enabled me to cut right down on painkillers.'
Julie, legal secretary

The physio's assessment of your condition

This is where the physiotherapist's training is very important. When you arrive for your first appointment at the clinic, make sure that the person you are seeing has experience in treating RSI, or is closely supervised by someone who has. Try to ensure you have access to the most appropriate skills in the clinic regarding your condition.

A good physiotherapist will be able to tell a lot about you from your posture – the way you hold yourself both when you are still and when you are moving. She or he will want to hear your history of symptoms and past injuries, if any. The normal range of your body movement – head and neck, trunk, arms, hands and shoulders – will be examined to seek out stiffness and tension in specific muscles, joints and nerves which you may not have noticed.

The choice of hands-on treatment will depend on what the examination reveals. The physiotherapist may deploy different types of manipulation, involving joint mobilization and massage. Three techniques which can particularly help RSI sufferers are as follows:

- *Mobilization of adverse neural tension*, also known as ANT or adverse neural dynamics, is used to free up so-called tethered nerves. Tethering or compression of a nerve is thought to result from its constriction when it passes through groups of tense, locked muscles, in turn causing the nerve itself to contract. Gentle stretching helps to ease the constriction and promote healing.
- *Trigger point therapy*, also known as myotherapy, is used to relieve muscle tension. The technique involves massaging tense knots of muscle and associated connective tissue (fascia) formed at 'myofascial trigger points'. These occur at numerous fixed locations in the body musculature, where they may store pain and tension referred

from other, sometimes remote, sites. Gentle massage can release both the trigger point and associated tension.

- *Muscle balancing techniques* are used to re-balance abnormalities in large muscle groups caused by sustained, awkward posture. The underlying theory is that if certain muscle groups are overused, others will be underused. Both sets will be mechanically disadvantaged – the overused ones tending to become tight, and the underused ones to weaken, thereby perpetuating abnormal posture. Muscle balancing involves strengthening the weakened muscles and stretching the tensed ones opposing them.

A good physiotherapist can do much more than manipulate muscle groups and nerves and give 'passive' treatments. An individualized programme of stretches for you to do at home will usually be developed, together with advice on rest breaks and exercise. Postural adjustment and body awareness may be emphasized. Physios who specialize in RSI will also be able to provide information on ergonomics, including body-friendly work-station equipment and its use.

'The [NHS] physio I went to was very good. When I first went to see her I couldn't even turn my head sideways – and after the first session I could do that. She also showed me neural stretches to do at home. The one bad thing was that I only got 10 minutes twice a week for three weeks, then once a week for about six weeks, then nothing. I'm sure I would have got better a lot quicker if I'd had more physio earlier on.' *Jo, graphic designer*

Physiotherapy can be a godsend for some people with RSI. In others, it can be of limited help – or even exacerbate the problem. And if it is helpful, it may well be short term: physios with the NHS usually only treat patients for a few weeks or months in the 'acute' stage of a condition. So even if the RSI improves markedly during that time, it is unlikely to clear up completely. Your physio will tell you to maintain your stretches and exercise regime for further progress – and these are crucial to recovery. But if you want the treatment to continue, you will have to go to a private practitioner.

It's not getting better. Please can I see a specialist?

After visiting your GP and undergoing physiotherapy, there may well come a time when your condition is not much improved and back you go to ask for another referral. There must be some specialist, you argue,

17

who can help. You may even have heard of one at a major hospital or clinic – and be willing to pay if your symptoms are still bad and you're desperate.

If your GP is supportive, a referral may transpire. But since there is no standard approach to management, nor consensus view on causes, RSI does not fall neatly into the domain of any one medical speciality, and you could be referred to any one of a variety of medical specialists. A recent TUC survey of RSI patients found that over 40 per cent were referred to two or more. The most popular were orthopaedic surgeons (65 per cent), followed by rheumatologists (43 per cent), consultant physicians (17 per cent) and neurologists (13 per cent). And the diagnosis and treatment any of these recommends may vary, depending on their speciality. You are more likely to be offered surgery by a surgeon, to pick an obvious example.

Specialist diagnosis: tests for RSI-type conditions

Since there is no established diagnostic test for RSI, the specialist depends largely on the clinical history to establish a diagnosis; that is, the symptoms, what may have brought them on, and any medical conditions or previous injuries that may be contributing.

He or she may well then order a number of tests designed to exclude conditions that mimic RSI. Pain in the hands and arms can be caused by several rheumatic diseases, including osteoarthritis, rheumatoid arthritis and systemic lupus erythematosus (more commonly known as 'lupus'), as well as non-rheumatoid arthritis. Exploratory blood tests will exclude these conditions, and an X-ray may help. About one in 20 people with presumed RSI have something unrelated, such as one of the above.

Once these conditions are excluded, and there is a diagnosis of presumed RSI or 'upper limb disorder', the doctor will probably look for definable pathological features of soft tissue rheumatism that may be contributing. These conditions are not the same as diffuse RSI, but they can look similar, or even overlap with diffuse RSI, so they are often confused with it. Some doctors include them under the wider RSI umbrella; others exclude them.

The most common are the following.

- *Lateral or medial epicondylitis*, popularly known as tennis and golfer's elbow respectively. This is inflammation of the connective tissue attaching to the bony projections (epicondyls) at the inner (median) or outer (lateral) edges of the elbow joint.

18

- *Tenosynovitis*: inflammation of a tendon sheath, typically involving the long extensor tendon to the thumb – De Quervain's disease.
- *Carpal tunnel syndrome*: compression of the median nerve in the carpal tunnel, the narrow passageway formed by the bones and ligaments at the wrist, through which nerves, blood vessels and tendons supplying the hand and fingers pass.

These specific, definable conditions are easily distinguished on the basis of specific clinical signs. For *epicondylitis*, this is pain on pressure to the epicondyl, and pain on movement that strains that epicondyl. For *tenosynovitis* it is a rasping sensation (crepitus) detected by the doctor on movement, and/or swelling over the particular tendon involved. For *carpal tunnel syndrome*, it is classically stimulation of pins and needles in the thumb, index and middle fingers on banging the median nerve in the carpal tunnel with a reflex hammer (Tinel's test).

Some element of one of these definable conditions contributes to the symptoms in a proportion of RSI cases: the exact proportion is difficult to tell since there are no reliable statistics.

However, many patients with RSI have no specific clinical signs. They emerge from the tests and clinical examination with a string of negative results. Everything looks normal. But as with specific forms of RSI, there will invariably be a clear tie-up between the symptoms and occupational factors such as a change in the person's job, workload or work equipment. These people have diffuse or non-specific RSI, and it is this condition with which this book is mainly concerned.

As previously mentioned, the difference between specific and diffuse forms of RSI is not clear cut. People with specific, diagnosable upper limb pain conditions can often have diffuse pain as well, or the specific condition may lead to diffuse RSI. So from the point of view of coping with a specific form of RSI, it is important not to rely on the treatment provided for that condition as a total solution, and put your head in the sand about postural, lifestyle and work-station changes you may also need to address.

Two other chronic pain conditions need to be mentioned. These are *fibromyalgia* and *reflex sympathetic dystrophy* – both of which can develop in people with RSI, as rarer medical complications of the condition.

- *Fibromyalgia* means, literally, pain in the muscle fibres. In fibro-myalgia, the chronic pain spreads over most of the body, left and right sides, above and below the waist, leading to exhaustion and disturbed sleep. As with RSI, it's not clear why some people get this rather than others.

- *Reflex sympathetic dystrophy* is a complex disorder involving the sympathetic nervous system, in which painful impulses seem to cycle around the affected area. There are a number of strange symptoms related to disturbances of blood flow and motor co-ordination, causing fluctuations in skin temperature and colour, sweating, and involuntary movements, alongside prolonged, continuous pain. Movement is restricted, leading eventually to muscle wasting (dystrophy) and further loss of mobility. The cause of this dreadful condition is obscure, though it can follow accidental injury and surgery, so trauma is a likely precipitant.

Specialist medical treatments for RSI

Treatment for definable RSI conditions – epicondylitis, tenosynovitis and carpal tunnel syndrome – is quite specific.

For epicondylitis, the preferred treatment is local injections of steroids, ultrasound or other physiotherapy; occasionally an operation is recommended if other options fail. For tenosynovitis, the most used treatment is infiltration of a steroid into the tendon sheath. These treatments give significant improvement in 30–40 per cent of cases first time around, though repeated treatments have a diminishing chance of success.

For carpal tunnel syndrome, the preferred treatment is surgery to relieve the nerve compression, with local steroid injections for people who don't want an operation. The success rate with this operation is somewhat higher, provided the problem really is confined to the carpal tunnel.

Surgery is only recommended in a minority of patients with RSI in the UK. Specific nerve compression – well-defined carpal tunnel syndrome, and very occasionally cases of epicondylitis and De Quervain's disease – can respond well to surgery, with reported success rates of 70–90 per cent. However, diffuse symptoms are unaffected and surgery is therefore inappropriate for diffuse RSI.

In the USA, a diagnosis of carpal tunnel syndrome, and consequent surgery, is far more common than in the UK. This may have something to do with North American patients being more insistent on a specific, technical-sounding diagnosis, and doctors being more eager to intervene. Thousands of pointless operations are probably carried out every year.

If you are recommended to a specialist who proposes an operation, think very carefully and take lots of advice before you make up your mind.

For diffuse RSI, particularly when it is established, it is generally accepted that both conventional medical treatments and surgery are invariably unsuccessful. More radical approaches are required.

Some specialists employ nerve-blocking injections for pain relief. This involves the injection of local anaesthetics near the spinal cord to block nerves at their roots, usually in combination with a steroid for its anti-inflammatory effect. A more common symptom-relieving strategy is prescription of tricyclic antidepressants (see page 13). With both these approaches for chronic pain sufferers, however, the same holds true as for other types of pain relief. The longer the pain has gone on, the less successful the painkilling treatments will probably be.

Overall, the value of symptomatic approaches for diffuse RSI, once it has become established, is extremely limited. This is because RSI is a chronic pain condition – simply that. There may, in the end, turn out to be no actual damage to the nerves or tissues – no 'injury', visible or invisible. It may just be that the pain itself has set up patterns in the tissues and nervous system that have become ingrained and self-perpetuating. *Whatever the pathology of diffuse RSI, the pain is the problem.*

Specialists in chronic pain management define diffuse RSI as just 'upper limb pain' or 'neuropathic arm pain' – pain in the arms related to a malfunction in the nervous system. By far the most successful treatment strategy that medical specialists have yet devised is management of this chronic pain. The techniques of pain management are taught at a number of pain clinics throughout the UK, and their application is largely dependent on self-help. Most of the rest of this book is about how to take this route.

Will I ever recover?

Whether or not you can ever recover completely from full-blown RSI is the subject of more controversy. People with the condition entrenched in their bodies over a long period can eventually become symptom-free and appear to be fully 'recovered', but most will remain vulnerable to a flare-up in periods of overwork or tension. Even those who believe that full recovery is possible accept that it is a long and slow process – years rather than weeks or months.

'I have found recovery slow and up-and-down. You have relapses when you stop doing the things you know will help because your symptoms have temporarily gone away. It's a learning process, and attitude has a lot to do with it. The difference between being "well" and being "ill" is very subtle, as are the changes you have to make.'
Richard, software developer

The speed and extent of recovery will to some degree depend on whether the RSI sufferer entirely abandons keyboard or mouse use, or other repetitive activity associated with the condition, or tries to continue with it in a moderated fashion. These people may prefer successful symptom management to 'full recovery' as their responsive strategy to RSI.

Only one study has set out to provide a clinical prognosis for RSI sufferers. This suggests that the mean time to recovery is four and a half years, with 36 per cent of patients recovering within three years after removal of the 'triggering factor'. No-one can say what the chances are for those who resolutely refuse to abandon the triggering factor – say, hands-on computer work – entirely. In a small minority of cases, chronic pain persists for ten years or more, in spite of all clinical efforts at pain relief.

The reality, as this chapter has set out, is that most conventional medical treatments are relatively ineffective for diffuse RSI. Indeed, surgery, injections, inadequate diagnosis, inappropriate physiotherapy and painkilling drugs, can sometimes end up making things worse. Even seeing a top specialist can plunge you into despair if, after all the tests, he tells you there is nothing much he can do. Failed treatments demoralize; they also keep the sufferer locked into a cycle of successive tests and treatments, looking for a medical cure. *Such a cure does not exist.*

RSI is a chronic pain problem, complex in origin, complex to understand, complex to treat, complex to resolve. The fact that medical technology cannot yet explain or cure it does not mean there is nothing to be done. On the contrary, the consensus among specialists in chronic pain syndromes, including RSI, is that sufferers can learn to manage the pain and significantly improve their state of well-being. We should not dismiss other medical treatments entirely. These may play a useful – if sometimes minor – part in a personal recovery programme. So may alternative therapies and techniques. These are described in Chapter 3.

3

OK then, I'll try the alternatives

Considering the complementary therapies

After you have accepted that there is something seriously wrong and that your doctor is unable to help very much, you may turn to the complementary and alternative therapies. But where to begin?

Many people with RSI start going to all sorts of therapists, out of desperation. Not only can this be hugely expensive – it is also very confusing. If you do start to feel better, you don't know which of your therapies is working. You are frightened to give any of them up, so you accept the potential waste of money, energy and time. This chapter aims to familiarize you with the various possibilities and help you work out which to try.

'You get desperate, and you will try anything. You don't know how long to give it. Four sessions? Longer? It's not working, but maybe you're not giving it a chance. You are very vulnerable to therapists discouraging you from giving up their treatment. I spent thousands of pounds, most of it wasted.' *Steve, university researcher*

You don't need to give up on conventional medicine to investigate other options. In fact, this is not recommended. Most alternative therapists are happiest working alongside a person's regular doctor – hence the term 'complementary' medicine. And if your GP is open-minded, he or she may want to stay involved – indeed, may even be willing to refer you to an alternative health practitioner on the NHS.

Basic information on the most widely practised and accessible of the alternative physical therapies is offered in the following pages to give you some idea of what you might be letting yourself in for. Bear in mind, though, that the rapport you develop with your therapist may be just as important as the therapeutic technique itself in getting you better. So whatever you choose, make sure you find a therapist whom you like and in whom you have confidence.

Manipulative 'hands on' therapies

The manipulative therapies are much the most popular complementary treatments available. Many of the basic techniques are now assimilated by physiotherapy and are among those most successfully used in the treatment of RSI.

Remedial massage

Massage is a good place for the RSI sufferer to start. Designed to relax knotted muscles and other soft tissues, it is likely to provide some relief from your symptoms. It should on the whole be a pleasurable experience, though it may be uncomfortable during and after a treatment to start with, especially if your muscles are very knotted.

> 'Deep tissue massage made a huge difference. On the first occasion my back was black, it bruised very easily. The therapist said my upper back and neck were like an iron suit. It took her weeks to loosen it up. But after eight weeks of going every week, there was a big improvement.' *Dave, computer programmer*

Solid muscles will require a deep tissue massage, in which the muscles are first softened by stroking, and then rolled and kneaded at a deeper level to release tension and dislodge stored toxins. Besides relaxing the body, the process stimulates circulation of the blood and lymph, to improve the supply of oxygen and removal of waste products.

Massage should be suitable for all levels of RSI, though if you have very severe symptoms, you may require more gentle and frequent treatments to start with. It can also prevent RSI from developing, or getting worse. Since many people's problems start in the neck and shoulders, massaging here can avoid problems building in the hands and arms. But even extreme muscle tension can respond well over a number of treatments. Moreover, loosening up the muscles through massage can help to put you in better shape both for stretching exercises and for other alternative approaches, such as chiropractic, acupuncture, and the Alexander Technique.

Massage therapists are often fairly well connected to other alternative therapists and may be able to recommend you to another practitioner for further treatment.

> 'I'm doing what people should be doing for themselves – loosening up their muscles for them. Then they can help themselves by exercising and movement. These will continue the action of the massage.' *Mary, massage therapist*

Osteopathy

Osteopathy focuses on the connection between the function and structure of the muscles, the skeletal system, and the joints, ligaments and connective tissue that bind them all together. Malfunctions are addressed through a variety of manipulative techniques, including massage, joint mobilization, high velocity thrusts and gentle releasing.

You should have no problem finding an osteopath: there are more than 2,000 of them in the UK. They view themselves as complementary to, and supportive of, conventional medicine. In return, they are well respected by most doctors, particularly in the treatment of back and neck pain. Indeed, some GP practices may be able to refer you to an osteopath on the NHS.

An osteopath is likely to look to the upper back and neck in treating RSI, since this is where the control of the blood and nerve supply to the limbs is centralized. Treatment will usually involve a combination of deep tissue massage to the neck, shoulders and arms, together with mobilization of the elbow and wrist joints, and perhaps some spinal manipulation or release techniques.

Osteopathy claims some success in treating RSI in its earlier stages. Really entrenched symptoms are less likely to be responsive. If it is going to work, you would expect to see signs of progress within three to four half-hour weekly sessions.

'By the time I got to an osteopath I was beyond the crisis point. I'd give her a lot of credit for freeing up my spine, and helping to increase mobility around the neck and upper back. The osteopath really knew her stuff, which gave me a fair bit of confidence. It was one of the better things I did.' *Jim, software technician*

Chiropractic

Chiropractic is closely related to osteopathy. Many of the techniques used are similar, though chiropractic traditionally has a stronger focus on the spine, and some practitioners will occasionally require an X-ray to confirm their diagnosis.

The fundamental difference is in the underlying philosophy. Chiropractors believe that disruption in body function and physiology comes about through interference with the nerve supply by dysfunction in the joints of the spine and extremities, while osteopaths believe that disturbances in the blood supply are at the root of functional problems. In practice it doesn't matter which explanation seems more convincing, since in both cases the manipulations are designed to realign the whole body.

Gentle spinal manipulations, manual traction and soft-tissue massage would be typical hands-on chiropractic treatments, along with advice on ergonomics, exercise, stretches, and the use of hot and cold packs. Some chiropractic sessions can tend to be quite short, depending on the practitioner: the first consultation might take half an hour to an hour, and subsequent ones 15–30 minutes. Again, the less chronic your symptoms, the more effective the treatment is likely to be, and the quicker it is likely to work. Very severe symptoms can take a lot longer to resolve, particularly if the muscles are too rigid or too tender to take manipulations to start with.

Chiropractic, like osteopathy, is fairly readily available, well-regulated and recognized by law. You may occasionally be able to get it on the NHS, via your GP.

Kinesiology

Kinesiology has its roots in chiropractic, but uses the fundamental principles of oriental medicine regarding energy flows and energy balance. Weaknesses in the muscles are thought to reflect energy imbalances in the body, which in turn appear as abnormalities in the function of different body systems and organs.

Kinesiologists employ muscle testing techniques – pressing down on a client's extended arm, for example, while she or he is sitting. Weaknesses are usually treated as they are found, using light touch techniques or finger pressure massage at appropriate points. The muscle is then re-tested to check that the correction has worked.

A kinesiologist will often recommend self-help techniques for use at home: for example, massage at acupressure points, or rubbing sore muscles at their sites of origin and insertion into bone.

Kinesiology is more likely to be helpful in the earliest stages of diffuse RSI, and in clients with more discrete sets of symptoms, as in carpal tunnel syndrome. As a general rule, if kinesiology is going to work for you, there should be a noticeable improvement after no more than three sessions.

Postural retraining techniques

Postural retraining techniques are designed to improve your awareness of your body and how you are using it. The Alexander Technique is the best known and probably the most readily available; Feldenkrais and Pilates are well worth considering if there are teachers or workshops near you (see Useful Resources, page 122).

Postural retraining techniques are not therapies. Rather, they are skills training, like learning to drive a car or play a musical instrument, though with postural retraining a person is learning how to use themselves. Their basis is that most adults misuse their bodies quite badly, putting a lot of unnecessary tension and effort into the simplest movements and postures – sitting, for example. Bad habits become fixed over many years, eventually resulting in pain and other disorders of the muscles and skeletal system. Postural retraining techniques aim to undo these bad habits by helping the body find its way gently towards good habits. This will usually involve bringing back into use muscles which have been underused, alongside decreasing the tension associated with overusing other muscle groups.

Although postural retraining techniques are physical, with the teacher working 'hands-on' with the body, they all require a high degree of psychological involvement. Indeed, it is possible to approach postural retraining from a purely psychological angle, using biofeedback.

The unfamiliarity of some of the ideas involved in postural retraining can be very challenging and does put some people off. However, the investment is often well worth while.

'Alexander lessons didn't cure my bad posture, but they made me notice all the things I was doing wrong, when I was sitting, moving, even relaxing. How when I would hold a pen I would crush it, and when I opened a door I would fling it open instead of pushing it gently. It gives you a way of noticing your bad habits, and then doing something about them.' *Jo, graphic designer*

Alexander Technique

The Alexander Technique is usually taught on a one-to-one basis. Lessons involve the teacher guiding the student to good use of the body using a very gentle, hands-on approach. Much of the time the student practises ordinary activities like sitting down and getting up from a chair, or walking in a straight line.

Much emphasis is placed on the correct alignment of the head and neck, and on 'not doing' habitual tensing. Alexander teachers want the student to re-learn lost harmonious body usage, rather than put effort into doing an activity 'correctly'. This can feel extremely strange, especially to start with.

Some teachers will offer a preliminary series of lessons, during which you can become acquainted with the Alexander Technique and learn the basic ideas. Each lesson will usually last half to three-quarters of an hour. If you want to learn the technique in earnest, at least 20, probably 30, lessons are required before your body begins to incorporate the results into daily life. So it does need a long-term commitment. However, many RSI sufferers have found it extremely helpful in promoting recovery and preventing relapse.

'The Alexander Technique is very gentle. It's not about striving, it's about thinking. The best exercise my Alexander teacher gave me was to hold my hands together, in a praying position, and think of the fingers lengthening. I now do that automatically every time I pause. When my RSI was really bad my hands were completely crunched up into a ball. Now when I'm relaxing, the fingers are long.' *Rosemary, university researcher*

Feldenkrais method

The Feldenkrais method aims to increase body mobility and awareness through movement. However, unlike the Alexander Technique, with Feldenkrais there is much less emphasis on the specific positions of head, neck, back, and other parts of the body, and the changes happen at a more unconscious level.

Feldenkrais practitioners believe that subtle movements of limbs and other parts of the body enable us to tap into an awareness of new options for moving and using our bodies. With time and practice, the repetition of these movements reprogrammes the brain. In the process, a sense of connectedness between the different parts of the body and the mind is reclaimed, as well as a sense of pleasure in everyday physical activities.

In the case of RSI, the Feldenkrais method can allow a person to break down old patterns of pain and – especially – immobility induced by pain, using pain when it does occur as a guide to moving more skilfully.

The method can be learnt both on a one-to-one basis and in groups – which may work out cheaper, especially if you want to continue with lessons for several months. Once the technique has been learnt, however, it is really a question of putting it into practice in your life, as is also the case with the Alexander Technique.

'I found Feldenkrais surprisingly powerful. It had an immediate effect which changed the way I worked at the keyboard, though it's hard to say exactly how. I've been doing it a couple of years now. The reason I'm enthusiastic about it is that it seems more helpful in achieving a permanent recovery, rather than just an immediate palliative effect.' *Richard, software developer*

Pilates

Pilates – pronounced Pil-ah-tees – is far more strenuous than the Alexander Technique or Feldenkrais: it involves exercising the muscles, both to strengthen them and to improve flexibility. This gives a healthy work-out in addition to increased postural awareness.

As in some of the martial arts, the exercises are slow, flowing, and co-ordinated with the breathing, allowing the student time to think about what he or she is doing.

Pilates initially aims to build up the deep abdominal muscles – considered the core of good posture. Though it takes a while to do this, a beneficial side-effect for most people is a flat stomach. The net result overall, as with the Alexander Technique, is that you become far more conscious of your body and the way you use it – again, perfect for the long-term correction of postural problems associated with RSI.

It is best to start with an instructor if you can, and allow six months to a year to absorb the basic principles fully. After this, practice is required three times a week or more in order to maintain the benefit. Group classes tend to be the norm for Pilates work, though not available in all areas.

Oriental and related techniques

Acupuncture

Acupuncture is part of the ancient system of traditional Chinese medicine. One of the most widely used complementary therapies in the West, it is now largely accepted and well respected by the medical profession, particularly for its use in pain relief.

The basis of acupuncture is radically different from that of conventional medicine. Symptoms of illness are regarded as signs that the individual energy or life force, known as Qi (pronounced chee), is out of balance. The aim of acupuncture is to restore this balance and thus promote health. Acupuncture is traditionally used to prevent the development of illness, believed to follow energy imbalance.

An acupuncturist reads a person's energy levels by taking pulses at the wrist. They often also look at the tongue to assess the general state of health. Energy is said to flow in 14 main pathways in the body – known as meridians – which can be accessed via acupuncture points. Treatment at these points restores the energy balance.

Treatment usually involves inserting fine acupuncture needles just below the skin. The needles do not generally cause pain, but patients can often feel a twinge as an acupuncture point is stimulated. The needles may be removed immediately, or left in place for 15–20 minutes to take effect.

An acupuncturist will sometimes use a technique known as moxibustion. This involves burning a dried herb on or above the skin, from where it is removed as soon as discomfort is felt. Stimulation of acupuncture points using finger pressure – called acupressure – is also sometimes employed, particularly with children.

Acupuncture treatment of RSI would usually involve manipulation or needling of tender points along the meridians, many of which coincide with myofascial trigger points (see page 16), to release tension and resolve pain. At the same time, an acupuncturist will address any underlying energy imbalance.

The success of acupuncture for treatment of RSI varies. It can be a very effective painkiller for some people – in others it seems to have no impact at all. It is usually necessary to have a few fairly frequent treatments at first to build up an effect. When it does work, the duration of the effect varies; some people find it wears off very quickly, while others find it lasts several days or longer, as treatment progresses. The response may well depend on what stage the RSI is at; very tense muscles may need to be loosened up first for optimum benefit.

'Acupuncture was fantastic at getting rid of the pain. The effect would last maybe a day or two, but I was doing a lot of other things as well: Alexander Technique, massage, and running every day.' *Jo, graphic designer*

Shiatsu

Shiatsu – Japanese 'finger pressure' therapy – derives from the Japanese form of acupressure. Treatment is in many respects like massage, but with the therapist working with the acupuncture points and meridians (see above), using the thumbs, fingers, palms, elbows, and even knees and feet to apply pressure to these energy lines.

Shiatsu is gentler than acupuncture, and no needles are involved. Treatment usually takes place at floor level, with an initial session lasting maybe an hour and a quarter to an hour and a half, and subsequent sessions up to an hour each. Self-help exercises may be recommended for use at home.

The effects of shiatsu are similar to those of acupuncture.

Reflexology

Reflexology, a type of foot massage, has its roots in ancient Chinese medicine. Like acupuncture and shiatsu, reflexology works with the principles of energy flow through the body, and energy balancing as vital for maintenance of health.

The energy channels of reflexology are different from those of acupuncture and shiatsu. For reflexologists there are ten channels, each relating to a zone of the body and having its terminal points in the feet. Reflexes in the feet are believed to correspond to all parts of the body, such that the entire body can be mapped onto the feet – the big toe represents the head, for example. Disturbances in the functioning of any body part or organ can be felt as tenderness in the corresponding point on the foot. Massage at these points will disperse accumulated toxins, unblock stagnant energy, and allow the body energies to come into balance.

Reflexology is said to improve the circulation of the blood and the functioning of the glands, and to relax and revitalize the whole system. In RSI, in theory, it can work on all potentially affected areas: the central nervous system, muscular and skeletal systems, blood and lymph circulation and the endocrine glands.

Reflexology sessions generally last around one hour, and a course of six to eight sessions is usually recommended, depending on the severity of symptoms and the length of time for which they have been experienced. If the treatment is going to work, some evidence of improvement should be obvious after about three sessions.

Homeopathy

Homeopathy, from the Greek meaning 'similar suffering', involves treating a person with a remedy which closely matches their disease symptoms and personality. Since this runs counter to current clinical wisdom, science is at a loss to explain how homeopathy works. However, it undoubtedly does work for many people, including young children.

In contrast to most conventional (allopathic) medicine, homeopathy is not designed to suppress or even attentuate symptoms. Instead, it is believed to work by strengthening a person's constitution, including their immune system, so that they lose their sensitivities to stressors, and become stronger and more able to achieve full well-being. The preparation of remedies involves diluting the active ingredient to such an extent that there remains only a trace of its essence, the theory being that this is enough for the body to pick up and work with. The remedies are, therefore, safe.

An initial consultation with a homeopath would usually last one and a half hours, at the end of which an appropriate remedy would be prescribed. This can be different for different people, as treatment is always individualized.

As with conventional medicine, a homeopathic remedy alone will probably not be enough to turn an RSI condition around. Homeopathic treatment will be most acceptable and easier for RSI sufferers who have already used it for other conditions, and are familiar with the principles.

If you want to try it for the first time, it is important to follow the management protocol prescribed by your homeopath, as well as taking the remedy. Improvement should be obvious within a few weeks or months, depending on the duration of symptoms, if the treatment is going to work.

Nutritional therapy

Nutritionists look at the whole body system to assess deficiencies in essential nutrients, which may be due to inadequate diet or physiological factors such as poor absorption from the gut. Treatment will involve advising on a healthy diet to replenish nutrients and decrease inflammation, as well as supplementation as necessary.

Many people with RSI will have vitamin B6 nutritional deficiency. It is not sufficient, however, to replace this with vitamin B6 bought over the counter, since treatment will depend on what is causing the deficiency. Moreover, replacement will require fairly large doses, which tend to leach other nutrients out of the system and therefore need backing up with further dietary supplements.

Prescription will be highly individualized. This may involve the elimination of inflammatory compounds, such as saturated fats, and the avoidance of universal stressors, particularly caffeine, sugar, white flour and alcohol, all of which deplete B6, as do hormone replacement therapy and the contraceptive pill. The use of natural anti-inflammatories may be recommended.

A nutritionist is also likely to advise a substantial increase in fluid intake. Not tea and coffee, which are dehydrating in themselves, but water, specifically still mineral or filtered water. Computer workers are particularly prone to dehydration from the electromagnetic radiation that comes off the machines. A large bottle of water – 1.5–2.0 litres a day – is sufficient to replace daily losses.

Nutritional therapy is by its nature long term. After switching to an optimal diet, a therapist would expect to see some improvement in the symptoms within three to six months. If you manage to keep the diet going, the improvements should continue as well.

Choosing an alternative therapist

Choosing an alternative therapist will partly depend on what is available near you. Your search may yield limited choice, but choose carefully nonetheless. *There's no sense shopping around for a magic cure for RSI – there isn't one.*

Different therapies suit different people, and it's a question of experimenting to find out which one is for you. The following checklist may help you decide.

- Take recommendations from friends and colleagues, especially fellow RSI sufferers. If these are unavailable, try phoning alternative health clinic(s) listed in the Yellow Pages under clinics and ask for advice.
- Try to work out with the help of existing medical advice what the seat of your problem is. Is it your neck? Muscular tension? Try one of the manipulative therapies. Do you feel your energy is blocked? Tired and exhausted? Consider acupuncture, shiatsu or reflexology. Bear in mind, though, that alternative therapies are all holistic in their approach, meaning that they all aim to promote overall health.
- Use your intuition. If one type of therapy particularly appeals to you, give it a go – at least for a while.
- The rapport you have with any therapist is probably as important as the treatment itself, since it will influence the benefits you get. Make sure your therapist is someone you like and feel you can trust, right from the start.
- Most important: check that whoever you pick is well qualified, and preferably has experience of treating people with RSI.
- Postural retraining and nutritional therapy are long-term approaches. With any other therapies, if you do not see at least some improvement within a few weeks and a few sessions – say four to six as a rough guideline – *leave*! Try something else instead.

- Postural retraining is a good long-term strategy for anyone with severe diffuse RSI. However, if you are very tense, you will probably need loosening up with one of the manipulative therapies first, just to allow you to start to become more aware of your body.

'When I went to Alexander lessons, the teacher was always saying: "Can't you feel the difference?" and I couldn't. We both got fed up with each other. She'd say: "You must learn to release your neck", and I'd try and try but it was meaningless. Now, because I'm much more in touch with my body, I can release my neck. What a huge difference it makes!' *Daisy, writer and editor*

- Try not to mix and match your therapies. Try one approach at a time. If you want to try two, add the second later. And if you do choose a combination, make sure it is a sensible one by discussing it with the practitioners first.

Pros and cons of alternative therapies

Alternative therapies can be both nourishing and fun. In sharp contrast to conventional medicine, they allow you lots of time with the therapist, and lots of attention. And they take a 'whole person' approach which is particularly appropriate with RSI. Plus it can be a great relief to feel that somebody is at last taking your condition seriously, if this hasn't been the case with your doctor.

However, these therapies can be expensive, and some practitioners can be con artists. *None is essential for your recovery*. The success of any therapy will depend to a large extent on your commitment to getting better. *You* need to put in a lot of work yourself, and therapy is not a substitute.

While alternative therapies may have a positive effect on RSI symptoms, therapies of any kind can best be seen as part of an overall management regime involving personal, working and lifestyle changes. Subsequent chapters describe the ingredients of such an approach.

One of the most important places to start is in the workplace, at the work station. That is the subject of Chapter 4.

4

What can I do about my work station?

Are you sitting uncomfortably?

Since postural problems are at the root of many people's RSI, a work station which is going to help rather than hinder is essential. Your table or desk, chair, computer monitor, mouse and keyboard are all important. Get any one of them wrong, and you are almost certain to acquire bad postural habits. Put it right, and this will help undo harm already done.

Most of us have unwittingly adopted a range of bad working habits which cumulatively affect our posture. Check out your own by taking a look at the way you sit at your desk. Are your feet flat on the floor – or tucked under the chair?

Are your shoulders raised and tense – even propped into this position – by arm rests on your chair? Are your hands higher than your elbows, forcing your wrists onto the work surface as you type?

Is the mouse placed off to one side so that you have to reach for it, bending your wrist out to the side as you do so? Is the monitor too low, or too high, so that you can't hold your head straight as you look at the screen? Or is it at an angle to the desk, so that you need to twist your body and cross your legs while you work?

These are some of the commonest errors, which over time entrench postural defects in the body. Good ergonomics can help correct the errors, and eventually help redress the postural habits which may be causing – or contributing to – computer-induced RSI.

Ergonomics is about optimizing the relationship between a person and his or her immediate physical environment. In the office, this includes work-station equipment, sitting posture and movement, work style and organization. It also includes stress-related environmental factors like lighting and noise levels.

Aside from workload, posture is probably the most important ergonomic consideration for the RSI sufferer. Sitting for long periods with the arms outstretched from the elbows is completely unnatural for the body. The muscles in the upper arms have to be continually tensed – what's known as 'static loading'.

During static loading, circulation is drastically reduced. Nutrients and oxygen can't easily enter the muscles, and waste products – lactic

35

acid and carbon dioxide, produced by muscle use – can't easily leave. Add to the static upper body picture crossed legs or feet, hunched shoulders and head poked forward, and you have a postural disaster.

Incorrect head positioning is particularly risky since the head is extremely heavy: the average head weighs 14 lb. Fortunately, the body is designed for the weight of the head to be supported through the neck by the spine. But this depends on all three being in the correct alignment. If your head is bent forward for prolonged periods to look at the keyboard, peer at the screen, or read papers on your desk, this automatically puts severe stress on the neck and shoulders.

A heavy workload, tight deadlines and a stressful work environment all combine to exacerbate physical tension. Constricted, repetitive movements of the hands and arms can be the final straw in overloading the system.

The problem is that bad posture is largely unconscious. Few people are aware that they are building up problems in their bodies by the way they are sitting and holding themselves – until the body takes retaliative action.

Factors that commonly contribute to poor posture

- Chair too small, too low (often) or too high (less often)
- Desk/keyboard too high (often) or too low (less often)
- Desk too small to hold all equipment and papers needed
- Computer off-centre on desk
- Monitor too low or too high
- Keyboard well off-centre, or set at an angle
- Mouse out of reach, and/or off to one side
- Work area poorly lit
- Text on screen difficult to read because of glare, or positioning of screen against window
- Elbows held outwards, perhaps due to overweight, so that wrists have to bend out sideways to centre over keyboard
- Long fingernails so that fingers can't slope down onto keys during keying
- Looking down at keys while typing
- Documents for reading and writing flat on desk, so that neck is frequently bent downwards
- Documents not at screen level, so head has to continually move up and down, backwards and forwards between the two.

'Bad habits change your body. Different muscles become weaker and stronger than they should be. Sitting slumped forwards using the computer and the mouse all day meant my shoulders were completely hunched, so that not even sitting back in a chair to relax was comfortable.' *Jo, graphic designer*

How can I get my work position right?

The first thing to remember about good sitting posture is that no fixed position is ideal. Some are undoubtedly better than others, but rigidly sticking to any one position will cause problems over time.

Human beings are not meant to be static. *Human beings were designed to move about and undertake physical action.* Our posture should accordingly be dynamic – with frequent changes in position, as well as standing up, moving around, reaching out, picking up, stretching, and so on. Shifting about in your seat on a regular basis is a really good idea.

You need to consider whether your work equipment is contributing to your problems. You may be able to get help with both assessment and costs through the government's Access to Work Scheme (see RSI, Your Employer and the Law, page 119). For a short list of suppliers of office ergonomic equipment, see Useful Resources (page 124).

Chair and sitting

The office chair is probably the most important piece of work equipment for the RSI sufferer to get right. It is vital that your chair provides good support and is sufficiently adjustable to allow you to sit comfortably. A high quality, ergonomically sound chair for VDU work is worth the money: regard it as an investment for your future health.

The perfect chair should be fully adjustable for your legs, your back and your height, and a tilt mechanism is recommended by many advisors for adjusting the angle of the seat.

'What does a fancy new armchair cost? It can easily be several hundred pounds. I sit in my office chair for far more time than I ever sit in any armchair. It's crazy to go on using some rubbishy thing and not invest in the chair that your working life depends on.' *Daisy, writer and editor*

You need to sit so that your feet are flat on the floor, in flat shoes, with the knees slightly apart. This spreads the upper body weight best between the sitting bones. Your upper body – especially the small of the back – should be well supported by the seat, so that your spine and neck are in neutral: i.e. in their natural, straight, self-supporting alignment. And there should be no excess pressure on the underside of the thighs or backs of the knees.

Once the height is correct, you can adjust the seat depth and backrest. Many people find it best at this point to adjust the forward tilt of the seat also, by around 10 degrees, so the hips are at a wider angle. This is thought to reduce pressure on the lower vertebrae of the spine, and provide a more natural alignment.

Some RSI sufferers find tilted kneeling stools, such as the Balans chair, very comfortable. However, an ergonomically designed chair will provide a perfectly sufficient degree of forward tilt, while avoiding excess pressure on the knees. It will also provide better support for your back, which helps to allow changes in posture. If you use a backrest, it will usually be most comfortable when adjusted to fit the lumbar curve of your lower back.

Arm rests are optional. It's best to avoid them if you find that they're pushing your shoulders up (because they're too high), encouraging you to slump (too low), preventing you from getting comfortably close to your table or desk (too long), or inhibiting the free movement of your arms during keying.

Once you've got a good chair, take the time to learn how to use it. Pay attention when you sit down, and check your posture frequently during the day – at least once an hour. It may help to use a 'posture mantra', say: 'Head soft, neck long, jaw loose, shoulders down, back straight, feet flat'. Or something similar.

Work surface height and area

Your office desk or table needs to be sufficiently high for you to be able to key comfortably with your forearms parallel to the ground, or slightly lower, and your wrists in a neutral position. There also needs to be sufficient clearance for the legs. Many older style desks were designed for writing and are too high for computer use. Best to change your desk, if this is the case, or use a footrest if that's impossible.

A height-adjustable table which can be raised or lowered for different tasks, or to suit different people working at the same desk, is another option. However, expense is a drawback. Moreover, you probably won't want to be adjusting the height of your work surface every time you change tasks, unless this is really infrequent.

If you do any quantity of paperwork as well as keying on a regular basis, you really need two work surfaces, that for keying being approximately 40mm lower than that for hand-writing, thus taking account of the height of the keyboard. A good arrangement is to have the two surfaces at right angles to each other, so that you can simply swivel in your chair when switching from one task to the other. An alternative is a keyboard tray, attached to the lower surface of the table or desk, so that it can be recessed underneath when not in use.

The desirable heights of the two working surfaces will depend on your body dimensions: lower leg length, upper arm length and trunk length will affect optimal work heights, even for people of the same standing height.

The surface area of your desk is just as important as its height. It should be sufficiently large to accommodate all the equipment you regularly use – keyboard, mouse, monitor, modem, document holder(s), papers, telephone, and so on – sensibly arranged, to work well for you.

Put the things you use most nearest to you. Your aim is to avoid any repeated awkward bending, twisting or reaching for items in common use, such as the mouse. (More on mouse use in Chapter 5.) Try to distinguish between these damaging kinds of equipment-usage habits and the need to stretch, move and shift position while at your desk.

Footrests

A footrest is simply a means of adjusting your height relative to that of your desk. It should be a standard piece of equipment for people less than 5'2" or 5'3" tall, but is also necessary when the desk is otherwise too high to achieve a comfortable, parallel forearm height.

Footrests can be purchased or constructed. A low wooden platform is ideal, and can be made larger than most shop-bought varieties, allowing greater flexibility in leg posture.

Off-the-shelf footrests are available that can accommodate foot-pedals for audio secretaries.

Keyboard and wrist posture

Your keyboard should be directly in front of you on the work surface, and at the correct height, as above. The general idea is that your hands should hover over the keyboard, with the wrists in a neutral position and the fingers naturally and relaxedly dropping downwards onto the keys. For the same reason, if you use a mouse it should be kept close at hand, not at the back or the side of your desk so that you have to reach over for it.

Wrist and hand posture are really important. Deviation from the neutral can be a major cause of soft tissue strain and nerve entrapment, particularly carpal tunnel syndrome. Two very common forms of misuse are bending the hands upwards and backwards at the wrist – termed wrist extension – and bending the hands sideways, towards the little finger – called ulnar deviation (see Figure 1).

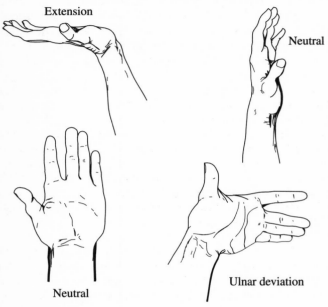

Figure 1. Wrist postures

Anyone who rests their hands on the desk while they key, or on a so-called wrist rest, is unwittingly practising wrist extension. Ulnar deviation can be a problem in broader people, brought on because they need to bend their wrists sideways to compensate for the elbows being relatively pushed out. It is particularly common, too, with right-handed mouse use. The design of the standard keyboard, with its right-sided numeric keypad, encourages many users to place the mouse way off to the right of the desk.

Monitor screen and head posture

The monitor screen should be directly in front of you, with the top of the monitor at eye level or lower. You need to be able to view the screen without twisting your body sideways or bending your head upwards or downwards and causing neck strain.

There is no correct 'viewing distance' between eyes and screen. But since the eyes are naturally more relaxed with distance viewing, placing the monitor as far away as you can within your comfort zone is usually the best option.

The monitor may need special adjustment if you wear bi-focals. Tilting the head back to look through the reading prescription at the bottom part of the lens can cause a great deal of strain and soreness in the neck and shoulders. A separate pair of spectacles for computer use that focus at the right distance for the screen is the ideal solution.

Lighting

Poor lighting is a prime cause of eyestrain, which can lead on to back strain, peering postures, and consequent tension in the neck and shoulders, which directly contributes to RSI. To minimize problems, it is important to avoid glare, both direct – that is, light shining directly into the eyes – and reflections.

There should be no shadows on your desk – check this using a pencil to highlight weaknesses in the general background lighting. Ideally, this should be diffuse. You can test for reflections by holding a small mirror up in front of the computer screen, to look at where reflected light is coming from. Then reposition your screen and desk as necessary.

One of the commonest mistakes is to sit facing a window for computing, so that your eyes have to accommodate to bright light in the background and the computer screen in the foreground simultaneously. Reposition the computer screen at right angles to the window. An anti-glare filter on the front of the screen is a second-best option. As a final resort, change the colours of the text and screen background. White or yellow text on a dark blue background is much easier on the eyes than the conventional black on white.

Use task lighting to illuminate paperwork on your desk. A flexible lamp is ideal for its adjustability, and bracketing it to the side of the desk saves it taking up valuable desk space. However, make sure to position your task light so that it doesn't produce reflections on the computer screen.

Getting into position

To achieve a good working posture at the computer, it is best to work from the ground up, as shown in Figure 2.

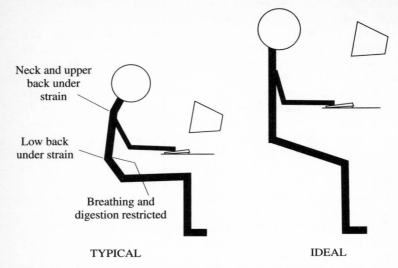

Neck and upper
back under
strain

Low back
under strain

Breathing and
digestion restricted

TYPICAL   IDEAL

Figure 2. Typical and ideal sitting positions for computer work. When the ideal sitting position is achieved, the back and neck are free of strain and the keyboard height, screen height and angle are correct.

Reproduced by permission of 'Alternative Sitting', Witney, Oxfordshire.

1 Make sure your *feet are flat* on the floor.
2 Adjust your *chair height* accordingly, with the seat horizontal. Once the height is correct, you can adjust the *seat depth*, the *backrest*, and the *forward tilt* of the seat.
3 Check that your *forearms* are parallel to the ground when positioned over the home key row on the keyboard.
4 If you've done steps 1–3 but can't get your forearms horizontal, it probably means that your *desk* is too high. Change your desk for one the correct height – or get a footrest.
5 Finally, adjust the height of your monitor *screen*.

What about gizmos and gadgetry?

Making sure that you have a good chair and adjusting the relative heights and positions of your various items of office equipment will prevent the ergonomics of your work station contributing to the development of RSI. But a number of techno-gadgets will allow you to go a step or two further in perfecting your work-station set-up. Important among these are voice recognition software, ergonomic keyboards and mouse alternatives, to be covered in Chapter 5. Several other items are worth considering. See Useful Resources (page 124) for suppliers.

Document and book holders

Some form of document holder is essential if you do any quantity of copy typing or paperwork at the computer. Free-standing and height- and angle-adjustable copystands on an arm that attaches to your desk are both available. Either kind should have a sloping surface at an angle of at least 45 degrees, preferably more, to bring the work up towards your eyes and prevent you developing neck and shoulder strain. They'll also have a rim or clip mechanism to prevent the papers from sliding off.

Documents are optimally positioned when they are at the same distance, height and angle as your optimally positioned computer monitor. Keeping the stand close to the screen will avoid unnecessary twisting as you switch your eyes between the two. A line guide can be particularly useful for data entry tasks.

If you frequently need to refer to heavier documents or books as you key, consider a free-standing copy-holder that will take both these and lighter papers. Alternatively, use a traditional book-stand or recipe-book holder which are sturdier; the latter are available from kitchen-ware shops and mail-order catalogues.

Writing slopes

Writing slopes are also extremely helpful for maintaining good posture if you do any quantity of writing by hand. An angle of 15 degrees is optimal. This will prevent curvature of the spine, and give good support for the hands and arms, with minimal risk of the copy sliding off the surface. For correct posture, a writing slope needs to be set up on a separate surface to that which holds your computer keyboard (see pages 38–9); or you need to raise and lower your chair as you move from one task to the other.

Keyboard/mouse trays

Some people find it more comfortable to type with the keyboard dropped down to a lower position. Check this out for yourself by putting your keyboard on your lap while you key for a short while. If it seems to work for you, you might consider buying a keyboard tray that bolts onto your desk, and retracts when not in use. Bear in mind that if you want to drop your hands for working, and you use a pointer device that needs a surface to operate, your keyboard tray needs to accommodate this too.

In setting up a keyboard tray, take care not to have it too low such that your wrists are bent forward in flexion, as this can also lead to problems. Follow the principle of keeping the wrists in neutral, with only the fingers dropped down (see Figure 1, page 40). You may need to angle the keyboard slightly backwards to achieve this.

'Putting the keyboard on my knees has been the best way of improving my use of it. The idea is to type with the force of each keystroke transmitted through the bones of the hand and arm, while keeping the shoulders relaxed. Relocating the mouse to a lower position, so that the mouse-using arm is down and relaxed when working, also definitely helped.' *Richard, software developer*

Wrist rests

Wrist rests should be treated with the same degree of caution as splints. They are really only helpful as a guide to keeping the wrists straight during keying or mousing. In practice, most types of wrist rests tend to restrict movement because of the temptation to rest the wrists on them while working. This can cause pressure on the carpal tunnel, and increase problems from ulnar deviation.

If you are going to use a wrist rest, choose a gel rest which the wrists will be able to slide over easily, without sticking. Alternatively, go for a height-adjustable articulated wrist rest which attaches to the side of the desk and supports the whole forearm. Avoid wrist rests that are too hard, too high, or made of rigid materials that in any way compress or restrict wrist movement. And never rest your wrists on a desktop wrist rest while using the keyboard or mouse.

Monitor arms

Monitor arms allow you to raise your computer screen to achieve a comfortable viewing height, and simultaneously create more space on your desk. Most also have a retractable keyboard tray that provides an out-of-the-way home for your keyboard when it's not in use.

In buying a monitor arm, it is best to go for maximum adjustability so that you can move the screen from side to side and front to back, as well as varying the height. Consider the weight of your monitor, too: standard monitor arms are meant for standard, 15" monitors; heavier equipment will require heavier duty support.

Take care that the screen is not too high – the top of the monitor should not be any higher than eye level. For most people, the lowest setting of the monitor arm will usually be right.

Telephone headsets

Consider one of these if you spend any considerable time on the telephone. Cradling the phone between the ear and shoulder while writing or typing is disastrous for the neck muscles and joints. Using a headset liberates the arms and hands for other work and avoids exacerbating already tense muscles.

'I first got RSI in 1990, and had to take several months off work. I didn't actually lose my job, but things got pretty unpleasant with my employer. I now work for a charity for disabled people and they've given me an ergonomic keyboard, a trackball mouse, and a wrist rest that clips to the desk to put my arm on. The work is mainly fundraising and telesales, which is much better for me than typing.' *Anne, former secretary*

Change your way of working!

No amount of work-station restyling or technological gadgetry will solve an RSI problem by itself. Your own input, both at work and outside it, is also needed. And attention is required to all aspects of the way you work – from typing technique to posture, workload to work practices. Good equipment will help, but *it can't do your job or change your posture for you on its own.*

'Technical gadgets are pretty useful, but you really have to look at the whole picture. It's no good changing your desk and chair and so on if you don't work at changing your bad postural habits.' *Jo, graphic designer*

You need to look at your working style, your work environment and the way you interact with it, and how you are subconsciously holding and using your body generally. You need to keep observing yourself and making adjustments until healthy work habits and good posture become second nature – just as bad habits were second nature until you developed RSI. This may seem obsessive at first – but it is essential.

Checklist for healthy posture

- Are you and your work positioned so that your head, neck and spine are in a neutral alignment – not bent forwards over the desk, or leaning to one side?
- Are your feet flat on the floor, with knees slightly apart?
- Are you sitting evenly on both sides of your bottom?
- Is your chair the right size?
- Is the chair backrest comfortable, giving good support to your lumbar curve when you sit back?
- Are your shoulders relaxed?
- Is your desk the right height – or do you need a footrest?
- Are your forearms and wrists parallel to the desk or sloped only slightly downwards when you are keying, with the wrists in neutral – not bent up, down, or out to either side?
- Are your fingers as relaxed as possible – not crunched up or splayed out?
- Do you use minimum force in striking the keys?
- Do you hold your pencils and pens lightly, with a minimum of force and tension?
- Is your monitor at eye level or lower, but not so that you need to bend your neck?
- Are the screen and text on it easy on the eye?
- Do you need a writing slope?
- Do you need a copy-holder?
- Is the mouse positioned so that you don't need to reach for it?
- Do you hold the mouse lightly and evenly, with your wrist in neutral – not resting on the desk, or bending out sideways?
- Do you change position frequently, and take regular breaks?

Workloads, work style

Workloads are rarely talked about in ergonomics textbooks or handouts, but they are one of the most important areas to address. After all, you can sit in a bad posture all day and get away with it if you don't have much work to do. By contrast, high keystroke rates can cause RSI in typists whose posture is otherwise perfectly good.

So if you've contracted RSI because of – or on top of – a heavy workload, this needs attention. You need to reduce the overall amount of work, often very considerably.

Your working style, general fitness, and the way you pace yourself at work are further key pieces of the ergonomics jigsaw. Taking breaks is really important, though easy to forget if you are deeply involved in your work. Systematic pacing is discussed in Chapter 8.

If your RSI is really entrenched, you will almost certainly need time away from the computer altogether. You can make good use of the break to investigate alternative ways of working, such as hands-free and hands-light computing. This is the subject of Chapter 5.

5

Making your computer work for you

Computers 'R' for us

If you buy a telephone or a TV, you have a huge range to choose from. Models come in different colours, shapes and sizes, and with many special features. Not so with computers. Computers come standard issue. There are PC clones or Apple Macs, and that's it. They come in beige or beige.

The keyboard is standard, and has the anachronistic QWERTY layout, designed in 1873 to slow down the user and prevent the keys from jamming. It suits right-handed touch-typists whose fingers are all the same length and whose arms extend from the centre of their chest. There's no separation of keys for right and left hand nor any consideration for the left-handed user. The numeric keypad is always on the right-hand side, and so are the cursor keys.

Whatever the reason computer manufacturers fail to provide the range of choice that we expect in other parts of our lives, the result is the same. We are expected to adjust to the computer – and we do!

We struggle to learn new software, switching from DOS to Windows and adjusting to using a mouse. And all too often, we compromise our posture and physiology by sitting hunched at the machine hour after hour without rest or exercise.

Common sense tells us that this is wrong. Computers are there to serve us – not the other way round. Many RSI sufferers have learnt the hard way that they've got this relationship wrong.

There are ways of operating computers that can make a big physical difference to your work life. They range from tuning your existing machine to purchasing more appropriate, hands-friendly and user-friendly hardware and software.

Customizing your keyboard

The standard keyboard and mouse are tuneable devices whose settings you can change in the same way that you adjust your office chair. Most computers have accessibility features which allow you to change the way you operate the keys. For older systems running DOS or Windows 3.1, access packs are available through AbilityNet (see Useful

48

Resources, page 127). Accessibility programmes allow you to increase or decrease the sensitivity of the keys. A 'sticky keys' feature allows you to hold down the Ctrl, Alt and Shift keys automatically, so that you don't have to press the second key simultaneously (e.g. Ctrl + B for bold). This avoids unnecessary twisting and stretching of the hands.

If you can't get on with a standard keyboard or think it could be to blame for discomfort, change it. There are many alternatives around.

Ergonomic keyboards

Ergonomic keyboards are designed to allow touch-typists to improve the positioning of their hands, fingers, wrists and forearms, through changing the design from the conventional. Many different types are available.

Split keyboards

Ergonomic keyboards generally involve splitting the keys operated by the two hands, to minimize ulnar deviation. One type of design slants the keys operated by each hand towards the respective elbow, either with a fixed angle or on a hinge. Another type separates the two halves of the keyboard so that the forearms are parallel.

Tented keyboards

An advance on split keyboards are tented varieties, where the centre keys are raised up relative to the outer ones. This modification is designed to reduce pronation of the forearms – the twisting needed with a standard keyboard to hold your hands with the palms facing downwards. Tented keyboards are invariably also split, and many are adjustable.

Scooped keyboard

The PCD Maltron is probably the best tested of the ergonomic keyboards. It is unique in having a scooped key layout to take account of the different lengths of the fingers, in addition to a split, tented design. The Maltron does cost around three times the price of other ergonomic keyboards, but you can try it out on a rental basis.

The Maltron keyboard can be purchased with a reconfigured, ergonomic key layout, or with the standard QWERTY layout.

'I first came across the Maltron keyboard at the local computer access centre. I had a go on it for half an hour that week and an hour the next, with minimal discomfort. After that, I decided to rent one. I persevered and the pains turned to aches, then the aches got less, and I could work for longer and longer. The difference from a standard keyboard is really marked.' *Ken, database administrator*

Other keyboard alternatives include the following:

Compact keyboards

These are around 60 per cent of standard keyboard size, thus saving desk space and allowing you to position your mouse closer to your body midline, where it's more ergonomic.

Reconfigured keyboards

These are standard keyboards on which the keys have been re-assigned by programming. The prototype is the Dvorak, designed to redistribute typing more evenly among the fingers of both hands, and thereby increase speed. (The fastest typists in the world all use the Dvorak layout). The benefit for RSI sufferers is that strain on the fingers, hands and wrists is reduced, since reaching for commonly used keys is minimized.

The Dvorak layout is supplied with Windows 95 operating systems and higher. Windows 3.1 can also be adapted using a diskette obtainable from Microsoft.

If you choose to reconfigure your keyboard you will need to re-label the keys. You may be able to replace the key tops. If not, you can buy plastic stickers from specialist suppliers.

Single-handed keyboards

A possible option for RSI sufferers affected in one hand only. But great caution is required because the additional use of the 'good' hand and arm may quickly cause symptoms to develop, especially if you have neck pain or stiffness.

PCD Maltron supply a keyboard for single-handed use, and there's a Dvorak programme for left-handed or right-handed use only.

Chord keyboards are probably the least stressful way to type fast with one hand. However, you have to learn a radically different technique for keying. They have only a few keys, which need to be pressed in combination, in a similar way to playing a musical chord on a piano. Left- and right-handed versions are available.

Modifying mouse use

Standard-issue mice are undeniably an ergonomic disaster, causing problems for large numbers of frequent users. The design is such that it encourages – even demands – deviant wrist postures. Problems will be exacerbated if the mouse is placed off to the right or back of the desk (see Chapter 4).

Prolonged gripping can cause difficulties too, particularly when this involves unnecessary tension. Many people fight with the physical movement of the device, and the rapidity of cursor movement. But double-clicking and dragging are probably the two actions that cause most damage.

You can improve your mouse use. Use the following guidelines:

● Do not rest your wrist on the desk while using the mouse. If this proves difficult, lower the mouse position or use a wrist rest – but beware pressure on the carpal tunnel (see page 44).
● Keep the mouse as close as possible to your body midline. If you're right-handed, try it some of the time in your left hand (you can switch the buttons over via the control panel software). Or rearrange your work station or desktop space to achieve this.
● If you feel that slowing the cursor down will be more comfortable, adjust the speed and acceleration settings under 'mouse properties' on the disabled-access menu.
● 'Mousetool' is another software solution, downloadable from the Internet. This will turn any mouse into a no-click device, with clicking being activated automatically depending on the cursor dwell time at its resting place.
● Keep your mouse *really* clean. Small judders caused by dirt on mouse rollers can cause disproportionate muscular tension.

Alternative mice

While standard mice are one-size and ambidextrous, others are designed specifically for the right or left hand, for small or large hands, or are sculpted to improve the positioning of the hand during use.

If you find clicking and dragging problematic, programmable mice are worth considering. With a three-button mouse, you can set the different buttons to click select, double-click, and drag lock (pick up and drop selected text). Four-button mice are also available.

Some devices have a wheel in addition to the buttons, enabling you to scroll up and down the screen.

Bear in mind that smoothness of movement and lightness of click can vary considerably between different models.

Alternative pointers

There are many alternatives to the standard mouse, including trackballs, styluses, touchpads, joy sticks, and foot-pedal mice (aka moles).

Trackballs are essentially upside-down mice whose working part – the ball – sits on top, so you don't have to grip. You move the pointer with your fingertips, thumb, or side of your hand. You can pick up the trackball, have it on your lap and move it from hand to hand.

Touch pads are operated by sliding a finger across the pad's surface to move the cursor. Tapping activates the click mechanism.

Graphics tablets look similar to touch pads, but involve moving a pen across the surface instead of a finger. The pen acts as a mouse, and the tablet represents the screen area. This allows for a high degree of accuracy, which makes these tablets suitable for artwork.

Some RSI sufferers find touch pads or trackballs helpful, but overuse of any device can probably worsen RSI. If the mouse is your bane, the best approach may be to have two or three devices and switch between them. An Apple Mac will support several such peripherals in parallel. With most PCs, however, you need to connect multiple devices via an external switch box such as a 'Mouser'.

For information and supply of special pointing devices and associated equipment, the specialist supplier is your best option. Or consult AbilityNet (see Useful Resources, page 127).

'I had two different mice at one stage – an optical mouse [graphics tablet] and a ball mouse. Certainly, using the pen stopped me getting mouse hand. I've now opted to use the pen all the time.' *Jerry, computer programmer*

The keyboard as alternative

If using a mouse hurts, the keyboard is your first and best alternative. This applies particularly to touch-typists who are already used to the keyboard. It's surprising how quickly you can learn to use Windows without a mouse if you just put it away in a drawer.

Almost everything you can do with a mouse, you can do on the keyboard via shortcuts. Look for the 'keyboard accelerators' – underlined characters on a menu item or button used in conjunction with Alt.

Pull-down menus give you other keyboard shortcuts, such as Ctrl + O for Open, Ctrl + S for Save, on the 'File' menu. You can use Tab to move from field to field within a function. Check shortcuts in Help.

'I'm convinced that mouse usage is a significant factor in the development of RSI. I learnt to use the mouse as little as possible. The rule is: when keyboard accelerators and keyboard shortcuts are available, always use them in preference to using the mouse.'
Richard, software developer

You can also create your own shortcuts. Frequently used text and graphics can be stored as macros – tiny programmes that can be operated from within an application to make everyday tasks easier. Most word-processing packages have very straightforward built-in macro facilities which you can learn to use with minimum computer literacy. All you need is the Help menu and a bit of time and patience.

Hands free: dictating direct to the computer

If you suffer from RSI, voice recognition software may literally save your career and your sanity. By allowing you to dictate straight into the computer and instruct it by voice instead of by hand, it enables you to bypass the keyboard and mouse entirely, if you want to. Or sufficiently to allow your hands and arms to recover – *if* you adopt an exercise, stretching and management regime – while you continue to work. For the RSI sufferer, this can give an enormous sense of relief and empowerment.

'VR for me was a transitional tool which allowed me to start work while I was still badly disabled. Over 18 months, I moved from using voice nearly all the time to using my arms nearly all the time. I also enjoyed it. The sheer delight of seeing the words come up on screen as I spoke them was just brilliant. Such a liberation!'
Frances, university lecturer

Voice recognition was spawned by a US defence project called ARPANET which was investigating voice activation of missile systems. IBM saw the possibilities and very soon started work on their own VR system. Dragon Systems soon followed, founded by two former ARPANET scientists, and IBM and Dragon remain today the two big names in voice recognition, though several clone software programmes have subsequently been developed.

Voice recognition today is software engineering at its most sophisti-cated. With a powerful computer, it will use every bit of processing power at its disposal. Operating in close conjunction with the soundcard and memory in the computer, it processes your speech into electronic data, compares it with that stored in the computer's speech data bank, and then converts it into text. All in a matter of microseconds!

Voice recognition software means that you can give your computer commands by speech, or you can dictate text straight onto the screen – assuming that it recognizes the words and your accent. Most programmes have a huge inbuilt vocabulary – up to 200,000 words – although they operate from a 'play pile' of the user's 30,000 most frequently used words. *You* train the system to recognize your voice, and it can build up a high degree of accuracy over time.

As far as accent is concerned, VR software can recognize anything from Cornish to Croatian provided it has been trained in your specific voice. You can add new words, proper nouns and acronyms too. Obviously the programmes are not word-perfect: they make mistakes – not spelling mistakes but confusions between words or phrases with a similar sound profile. However, there are inbuilt correction facilities, and the accuracy is continually improving as the systems develop and more powerful computers make it possible to deliver high accuracy.

'The software learns as you use it. I got one of the first packages to come out, and initially the recognition was very poor. But every time you correct a mistake it stores that correction. Now I can sometimes dictate a whole page without any mistakes at all.' *Peter, bank manager*

Choosing a voice recognition package

Choosing a VR software system can seem like negotiating a maze. The possibilities will depend on the severity of your symptoms, the depth of your pocket, and whether you are able to get help from the Employment Service and/or your employer. People with RSI are usually able to take advantage of the government's Access to Work Scheme, both for technical advice and for help towards equipment costs (see RSI, Your Employer and the Law, page 119).

Whether you are eligible for a government grant or not, it's a good idea to do your own research on VR. Start by asking yourself a few questions.

Checklist for considering VR software purchase

- What is your budget?
- What do you want to use VR software for?
- Will you need to run it on something other than a PC?
- Will you need to use it at more than one computer?
- Where do you want to use it?
- Will you need training and back-up support?

The question of cost

Although VR software is inexpensive to buy off the shelf, you need to be aware that this is only the beginning of its cost. For voice recognition to work effectively, you need to meet four basic requirements: the right VR software package; the right computer set-up; a compatible soundcard; and a high-quality microphone.

Meeting these requirements will often mean that you need to upgrade your system before you can expect results. There is a general rule for purchasing a computer set-up for use with VR software. *Get the most powerful machine you can afford, with the largest memory and the fastest speed.* The minimum requirements listed by the software manufacturers are much too low for effective speed and accuracy. And an inadequate computer set-up will not only slow you down, it will also be much more prone to system crashes.

A high-quality microphone and a good soundcard are as important as getting the computer and the software right.

Microphones

Since VR software suppliers have focused on trying to keep their costs low, the microphone and headset assembly supplied in the software packs may not be top quality. You may need to get a better mike to get good results. If so, consult with a specialist in speech recognition, and make sure the microphone you get is robust.

A really good mike should be comfortable, and should last for years. Your best bet is probably a lightweight headset, which is hardly noticeable when you're using it, and – once you have set it to the right position to dictate into – can be taken off and put on without major adjustment every time.

Soundcards

It's not necessary to spend money on a special soundcard. The top-range ones are more concerned with improving sound output than improving sound input – which is what you are interested in. For acceptable voice recognition, the soundcard in your machine just needs to be compatible with your VR software.

If you're buying a new computer, check with your supplier that the soundcard will be suitable – don't take it for granted. Unfortunately, many hardware manufacturers install cheap, inferior quality sound-cards, or place the soundcard too close to the power supply, creating a high level of noise disturbance – a particular problem with laptop machines.

If you have either one of these problems, you won't even be able to get your VR system off the starting block. When you try to sign on it will keep coming back at you with 'unacceptable sound quality'. To make sure everything will work, it is best to purchase computer and software together, from a specialist supplier (see page 126).

The two types of VR software package

VR software packages are of two basic types: discrete speech products, which recognize one word at a time; and continuous speech products, which allow you to speak in phrases. Discrete speech is awkward and something of a knack. To. Speak. One. Word. At. A. Time. Is. Quite. Unnatural. However, it becomes easy with practice. Both are very accurate (95 per cent plus) once trained.

All VR systems allow you to do word-processing by dictation. However, continuous speech products have two distinct advantages in this department: speed and comfort. Continuous speech products allow you to dictate at a relatively normal speaking rate – about 150 words per minute as opposed to 60–80 with discrete speech recognition. It is still not conversational speech, but it is an advance on the robotic diction you need with discrete speech packages.

Discrete speech products have advantages in other areas. They are the only products that will cope with really poor speech, for example a severe speech impediment. But for people who are not voice-disabled, the big plus is their command and control capabilities. Unlike continuous speech products, they allow you to control other applications by voice, e.g. send e-mail, use the Internet, or write software. They are much the best suited for applications other than word processing.

'I've written tens of thousands of lines of programming with VR software. But you need time to adapt the system, make use of macro and scripting language. I've changed my programming style to use words instead of letters because words – especially long words – are easier for it to recognize.' *Jerry, computer programmer*

Different horses for different courses

The next questions are: What do you want to use VR software for? And how do you want to use it?

The IBM and Dragon packages have two key differences. One is the correction system; Dragon's seems slightly more user-friendly. The other is that the IBM programmes require that you use your hands a little, whereas you can use Dragon products entirely hands-free: their discrete speech package – DragonDictate – was designed with the seriously disabled in mind. However, if you want to undertake functions other than word processing hands-free, you will need Dragon's discrete *and* continuous speech products.

'VR saved my career. But to use it completely hands-free would be pretty tedious. So I use it interactively: some talking, a little typing. It takes the load off the keyboard, which is very important.' *Steve, university researcher*

To decide between a discrete and a continuous VR software package, you need to analyse what you do during the working day. If you're involved almost exclusively in programming or design, you will need the command and control capabilities of a discrete speech product, but may have little use for continuous speech recognition.

If your primary need is to write text, and you can manage some keyboard use, you should be fine with one of the dictation-only, continuous speech recognition packages.

If you make regular use of two or more applications, do a fair amount of word processing, and want to switch between applications by voice, you should consider getting both continuous speech and command and control facilities.

Using VR with computer systems other than the PC

Most available VR systems have been developed for use on a PC. Apple Mac users will not have to agonize about what package to choose – there is only one Apple Mac VR software package available at present, PowerSecretary. It uses discrete speech.

It is possible to adapt VR software to run with Unix, Wang, AS400 and other operating systems by voice, with input from a specialist supplier. It can likewise be adapted to work with in-house mainframe systems and computer networks.

If you constantly work on two or more systems, you may be best off with a laptop instead. Otherwise you will need either to train the different systems separately, or to transfer the speech files between them – not something you want to have to do on a regular basis. Bear in mind, however, that laptop machines which haven't been supplied from a VR specialist can work poorly with VR software because the soundcards are often set up in a way that makes them less good at 'hearing'.

Another option is to purchase a customized dictation machine. You can then record text out of the office and transcribe it later using voice recognition, by plugging it into the back of your computer.

Training and back-up support

It's important not to underestimate the value of adequate training and support. As little as half a day's training will enable you to be up and running with reasonable accuracy, and can save you hours reading the manual or consulting the online help. If you haven't got the budget for training, try at least to see a good demonstration.

Any good specialist VR supplier will be able to provide both training and after-sales support. It may be that you have a friendly and available IT support person where you work, who is interested enough to help you get the most out of the new software. If not, it is worth investing in a back-up support contract with your supplier.

'The support system was really important. Trying to gen up on a new technology is the last thing you need when you're unable to do even basic things like hold a cup of tea. If I'd been on my own I don't think I'd have got it going.' *Frances, university lecturer*

So what are the drawbacks of speaking to your computer (apart from people thinking you're mad)?

For all its techno-wizardry and life-saving potential, VR software is not a magic wand that will miraculously solve all your problems. It can bring you back from the brink of a crisis, and be your ally while you recover. But it carries its own special challenges and risks. Expense. Frustration. And the risks of computer crashes and chronic laryngitis.

'I remember many pitfalls. The annoyance of wearing the headset, the ease with which extraneous noises could cause gibberish to appear on the screen, the length of time it took to make corrections, and the programme's maddening obsession with American presidents, e.g. "Nixon" for "mezzanine", "Reagan" for (Prince) "Regent".' *Tim, research historian [Note: British English versions and noise-filtering mikes are now standard]*

Expense

Most people purchasing VR software for the first time will need to upgrade their computer system to run it effectively. There really is no way around this.

If you can't get a grant and need to restrict your costs, a discrete speech product will probably be your best option. These will run very effectively on a Pentium 100 machine with 16 or 32 MB RAM. (They can even be made to work on a 486 – though this will be much slower.) Continuous speech products, by contrast, need a fast Pentium processor to work really effectively – a minimum of 266 MHz with 128 MB RAM.

Trying to cut corners on costs will invariably be a false economy. *A specialist supplier is always the best option for both hardware and software*, preferably bought as a combination package.

If you want to avoid headaches, don't buy a VR system from a high-street chain. Don't even buy it from a hardware supplier who claims to have fitted it before. There's a 50:50 chance you'll get a duff set-up – the wrong soundcard, or insufficient memory. And you won't have the technical back-up when your supplier claims it's not a hardware fault but a problem with the software.

Frustration

Closely allied with expense is frustration. Off-the-shelf VR software should really come with a health warning. Hours and hours of frustration, free with every pack!

Take advice from a specialist supplier on both the VR package and the computer upgrade to go with it. Otherwise, you could waste a great deal of time and money just getting it off the ground, and still fail. Many people – probably most – who buy VR software never get it working properly; they simply junk the package in frustration within a few weeks. Fortunately, this is completely avoidable with the proper advice.

Having got the right system, there's one golden rule: *Train, train,*

train. Take the time to 'enrol' your voice initially. For continuous speech products, this means 30–45 minutes' reading from *Alice in Wonderland* or some such classic text. (Not so easy in dictation mode, when you have to speak as if you're reading a report!) Over the following few weeks, do *all* the training exercises. Make full use of each package's special features. Use the vocabulary builder. Teach yourself how to write macros – or ask your supplier or computer enthusiast colleague to set them up for you. Every successful VR software user will tell you the same: taking the time to train your software really does pay dividends.

'My VR software was really good. But you do have to stick at training it. [My partner] was fantastic, and we learnt lots of Applescripts [macros] together. For a year I used it constantly and didn't use my hands at all.' *Jo, graphic designer*

Risk of laryngitis

Overuse of the voice – by anyone – carries a risk of chronic laryngitis. This is why actors and singers, who use their voices professionally, get proper training in how to use them. Talking for an hour or so uninterrupted is just not normal usage – it will take its toll.

There is also a view that people with computer-related RSI can be more prone to getting serious problems with their voice using VR software than others. This rings true simply because RSI sufferers seem to have a greater tendency to hold stresses in the upper body, including the neck and throat area.

So use your common sense with your VR software, and don't rush into it in a fit of enthusiasm. Find a really comfortable sitting position and talk as normally and relaxedly as possible. Be certain that the mike settings are high enough to avoid having to raise your voice as if your computer was deaf. Start with relatively short periods of use and build up. As with the keyboard, take breaks to get up and stretch. And keep a drink handy to avoid getting a dry throat. Above all, if you feel yourself getting tense using VR, *stop*!

Risk of crashes

Because VR systems are such big pieces of software, they can cause your hard disk to become volatile and crash. If the computer specifications are right, you shouldn't have crashes. But if you're light on memory or you run the programme with many others simultaneously it's a risk. Likewise if you upgrade either your computer or your VR software.

If you are dependent on VR software and your system crashes, the greatest casualty could well be your voice files. *You must back up your voice files on disk.* Otherwise, you face the prospect of starting again from scratch. You need a zip file or tape back-up – floppy disks won't be big enough.

Difficulties in an office environment

Noise and lack of privacy can be major issues if you share an office. Leading VR software nowadays is supplied with a quality, noise-cancelling microphone which sifts away background noise. However, short, sharp, shock sounds, such as the phone ringing, for example, can lead to garble in your document. Fortunately, it is possible to train the software to recognize and ignore such extraneous noises. A bigger problem is disturbance to and from other people. VR system users can feel embarrassed and inhibited about using the software, even when their colleagues don't complain.

If you work in an open plan office, investigate the possibilities of moving to a separate room or a quiet corner, or installing acoustic partitioning boards or moveable screens to reduce disturbance both ways. If this is impossible, you might consider getting a portable machine that will allow you to work from home for at least part of each week.

'Several people at work have tried it. The perceived opinion is that it doesn't work well within an editorial environment. A noise-free environment is needed and newspaper offices tend to be open plan.' *James, journalist*

For most RSI sufferers, VR software will be an excellent aid to recovery rather than a permanent solution. In the longer term you need to reclaim the use of your hands and arms. And for this, no amount of get-round technology will be adequate. You need to find a way of managing your pain problem and recovering your well-being. This is the subject of Chapter 6.

6

Beginning to get on top of the problem

The road to recovery

From everything we have seen so far, there is really one conclusion. If you are a chronic RSI sufferer, or heading that way, a doctor, a therapist, a new chair, various gadgets of various sorts, may help relieve your symptoms. But they are not going to provide 'a cure'.

By all means, take advantage of what's out there. New aids constantly come on the market which enable some of the human activity triggering your pain to be substituted by mechanical or electronic activity. Computer aids have become an industry, as we've seen in Chapters 4 and 5. There are many others. Foam holders to attach to a shopping trolley, bicycle handles or the wheel of a car to widen the grip and make it more comfortable; stands to hold up books and newspapers to spare arms from fatigue; electric carving knives, food processors and choppers which displace pressure or repetitive movement around food preparation; special openers for bottles and jars requiring 'grip and twist' movements. All these and many other gadgets can help.

Similarly, new devices claiming to relieve pain – a new analgesic combination drug, a new electrotherapeutic instrument – turn up in catalogues and in the stores. The wedge cushion or postural pillow may sound as if it has been invented with you in mind.

It is true that technology, whether of the medical or other kind, can do things for you. But frankly, not enough. At the end of the day, what you want to do is to *get better*! Most people, RSI sufferers included, don't want to have to prop up their lives – professional or domestic – on technological gadgets and medicine indefinitely. And no device is a substitute for getting on top of a chronic pain condition and being able to lead a normal life again.

'This disease is really serious. If you have it, then *panic*. When you have calmed down, get very serious about changing your lifestyle to deal with it.' *Richard, software developer*

The hard truth is that the only agent who is going to be able to make serious inroads on what is happening to you is you.

This does not mean that you are simply going to have to give up for ever the life you led 'before RSI'. It does mean that you are going to have to take ownership of your condition. You are almost certainly going to have to become your own primary 'therapist' and introduce significant changes into your life. Some of these changes will take time to have an effect. You will need courage, faith, and perseverance. And kindness towards yourself.

When you are in pain, or in despair, the last thing you want to hear is that recovery from this dreadful situation is all up to you. There is an immense psychological barrier to be overcome. One of the strongest human instincts is to want someone else to take the load away. And in the case of most illness, we are used to ever more sophisticated technological solutions being invented to do just that. But there is no such solution for conditions of chronic pain. That is an unavoidable fact. It is a fact that certain medical practitioners are doing their best to address. But for the time being, it is a fact we have to live with and work around.

It may seem frightening at first, the idea that you – not your doctor, not your therapist, not your counsellor, not your employer, not your partner – are going to be in charge of managing your condition. Don't worry, you can take it step by step. And when you think about it, you have probably already begun to assume some control over your condition – for example, by reading this book.

Chronic pain conditions can be 'managed'

Chronic pain conditions may not be susceptible to 'cure', but they are susceptible to 'management'. The theory of 'pain management' is simple. The idea is that if you can develop and put into practice your own regime of interlinked mind and body activities, you can make a significant impact on your pain condition. In the case of RSI, many of these activities also have a direct bearing on the tensed muscles and confused neural pathways that are making your arms and upper body ache.

In time, improved well-being and outlook may mean that your pain is significantly reduced, and/or that it simply doesn't bother you in the way it did. It may even improve to a point where it is a relatively minor irritant, and you can lead a fully normal, active, working life again. Yes, you will probably always have your 'weak spot': where someone else has a tendency to catch colds or twist their ankle, you may have a tendency to sore arms and a stiff neck. There will undoubtedly be flare-ups and setbacks. But you'll have more confidence in dealing with them. They won't be so frightening and they'll probably last for a lot shorter time than they used to.

Medical specialists have developed systems of 'pain management' drawing on a number of different disciplines. There are programmes in different parts of the country, some available under the NHS, whose two- and four-week residential courses include sessions by physiotherapists, occupational therapists, and psychologists. The approach suggested here draws from these systems, emphasizing those elements which are particularly appropriate for dealing with RSI.

'I went for a four-week pain management programme, and it changed my life. My RSI had even affected my legs – it pervaded my whole body. I went into the programme in a wheelchair, and I came out walking.' *Frances, university lecturer*

Managing RSI, or any non-specific pain condition primarily associated with computer use, requires the following:

- Two 'Fs': Fitness and Flexibility
- Two 'Ps': Pacing and Postural retraining
- Two 'Rs': Relaxation and Reinforcement

Each of the six components is closely interlinked with many or all of the others. Any successful pain management regime will require a balance between them. You should not opt for 'fitness', for example, and ignore 'relaxation'. And some are integral to others: 'pacing', for example, will apply to how you set about achieving greater 'flexibility' and other personal goals. 'Posture' will slump where there is no 'fitness'. And if you don't build in 'reinforcement' all the way down the line, your good intentions to carry out your new pain management regime may collapse after only days or weeks.

The subsequent chapters in this book explore these components in more detail, with more specific guidelines for what to do. Here, the rationale behind each of the components and a brief overview is provided.

The six components of computer pain management

Fitness

Many people with RSI or any other chronic pain conditions cut down on certain activities. This may be because that activity directly exacerbates their pain – playing the violin or embroidery in the case of

RSI, for example – or because they have little energy and are constantly tired. This leads to a loss of fitness, strength and flexibility in muscles and joints.

Some people feel forced by their pain to take life so carefully that when they try to do anything strenuous – carry shopping, go for a walk – their body complains that they are overdoing it, the pain gets worse and they become extremely discouraged. This, in turn, adds to their sense of frustration and despair.

Building up fitness and physical well-being is absolutely essential to managing pain. A fitter body is more able to combat symptoms and drive out pain, and a sense of physical well-being lifts mood and outlook. Exercises which will help you to do this safely are given in Chapter 7.

Flexibility

For RSI conditions, flexibility is as important as fitness. As we have seen, many sufferers' pain condition is connected to holding the upper body and limbs in stiff, cramped, tense positions for long periods of time over a keyboard or other equipment.

Stretching and flexing is needed to counteract whatever damage this has caused and continues to cause. Muscles and joints need to be moved regularly throughout the day. Fibrous tissues, which may have developed during a healing process, need to be elasticized. Stretching the soft tissues systematically may also help re-educate jangled nerves which have got into the habit of transmitting unhelpful pain messages.

Yoga is a particularly helpful way of both stretching and strengthening the body, and it has the additional advantage of helping you tune in to your body. Or you may prefer one of the other exercise systems which has a similar mind–body approach, such as T'ai Chi.

A set of stretches is given in Chapter 7.

Pacing

Pacing is central to carrying out an RSI management regime. It is not just 'don't push yourself', 'a bit at a time', 'take regular breaks' – although it does contain this kind of common sense. Pacing in a very systematic manner allows you to raise your capacity to do things incrementally, helping you to overcome pain-imposed limitations on your life by gradually re-educating and retraining your body and mind to do things pain-free.

Pacing applies to other parts of the regime – the fitness programme, for example – and to general activities with which you are experiencing problems. To be most effective, it needs to be practised using specific pacing techniques. These are the main subject of Chapter 8.

Postural retraining

Chapter 4 showed how important it is to set up your work station in such a way that potential postural problems are minimized. But many RSI sufferers also need to do something about the much more problematic side of the equation – the unhelpful way they are holding and using their bodies while they are employing this workplace equipment.

If you have already sought help from a physio or chiropractor, you may have been given specific exercises which address your own postural alignment needs. They may well overlap with exercises and stretches given in Chapter 7, since you cannot re-align your posture without loosening and strengthening your body first. You may also have chosen to go to an Alexander teacher, or to one of the other postural retrainers (see Chapter 3).

The way we hold our bodies is deeply ingrained – it has been learnt over our whole lifetime. Our bodies are like papers or fabrics which have been folded one way so often that they fall into the same pattern automatically. When you sit at your desk, stand over the stove, watch TV, your body takes up its own 'natural' position. But this 'natural' position may be a major contributor to your problem. To make any significant change in it will probably require more than a set of exercises and stretches, however rigorously carried out.

'Every week, I go to the gym for a work-out. It helps me enormously. You feel in tune with your body. The best thing I have learnt is knowledge of my body and how to use it. I have begun to realize that certain tasks – like being on the phone for ages – cause me problems unless I change the way I do them.' *James, journalist*

You may have to develop the habit of 'thinking Posture'. Thinking Posture does not mean putting yourself into some new, rigid, 'correct' position reminiscent of an Edwardian cartoon. It means taking a deep breath and saying to yourself every now and again wherever you are, at your desk, lying in bed, walking down the road: 'What are my shoulders doing?' 'Where is my chin?' 'Is my jaw or throat clenched?' 'Have I drawn my neck in like a tortoise or is it long like a swan?'

Just taking the breath and having the thoughts will tend to relax your muscles and send a signal to your body to make its own minor adjustments. In time, the sensation of bodily adjustment and realignment may become much more profound. And the body should begin to abandon its ingrained habits, falling into its old folds much less frequently without needing to be prompted. More about this in Chapter 7.

Relaxation

The word 'relaxation' covers both physical relaxation – the need to take rest breaks and time off from work – and mental relaxation. You may need to consider your relationship with your work and whether obsessive preoccupation with output or achievement is contributing to stress which is ultimately manifesting itself in pain.

A considerable number of computer pain sufferers develop RSI after a long and intensive spell of work in which they fail to take breaks and acknowledge warning signs. Moments of rest and relaxation can be built into the busiest schedule, and it is essential to do so. And to use time away from the workplace – weekends and holidays – to refresh your body and mind fully.

If you find it very difficult to relax, it is important to learn how to do so, and to build into your pain management regime periods in which you practise relaxation. Techniques for doing this are covered in Chapter 9.

Reinforcement

When you are trying to develop new skills and take your life in new directions, it is useful to build into the process a system of reinforcement. Reinforcing whatever progress you make is a positive and helpful coping strategy.

At a superficial level, reinforcement may simply mean giving yourself a treat for carrying out your regime: a chocolate for completing the full complement of stretches or a helping of your favourite book or video for devoting a half-hour to proper relaxation. This is a perfectly sensible method of reinforcement on a daily basis.

Setting yourself longer-term goals – to be able to play your violin again for 30 minutes a day, or be able to use the keyboard again for 10 minutes every morning and afternoon – is a very important part of your longer-term pain management regime. Working towards such goals, with a really motivating prize such as a weekend away, is another method of reinforcement. More about goal-setting in Chapter 9.

Another aspect of reinforcement is planning the various parts of your RSI management regime in such a way that you actively encourage yourself to carry them out. Many sufferers religiously carry out stretches and exercise programmes at the height of a flare-up. But when their condition improves, they lapse. Their symptoms swiftly reappear. So they get into a cycle of crisis → action → improvement → inaction → crisis. Ways of building in reinforcement to stop this happening are suggested in subsequent chapters.

How long will I need to carry out this regime?

If you have already been suffering from RSI for several months or longer, and you want to continue to work using a computer or whatever other activity triggered the problem, you are likely to need to carry out an RSI management regime *for the next several years*. In fact, you may well decide to use a modified regime for the remainder of your working life.

This is not a prison sentence – far from it. You will probably come to look on it as a liberation.

Things may be different if you leave work altogether, or manage to go into a totally different kind of job. But even if you do manage to organize some quite major workplace changes – for example, self-employment, or a job where you don't need to spend so much time at the keyboard – you will probably need a management regime *as well*.

Taking time off work – extended sick leave or a holiday to give your arms a break – is not a substitute for an RSI management regime. It is an opportunity to develop such a regime and start experimenting with it.

The ingredients will be the same, whether you are looking for 'prevention' or 'recovery'. The difference will mainly lie in the amount of time devoted on a daily basis and the emphasis given to different components.

Prevention management: A prevention regime suitable for those with preliminary symptoms would require that you spend 1–2 hours every day carrying it out, as well as making some changes in your working practice and personal life.

Recovery management: A more comprehensive regime, suitable for a chronic sufferer, requires more planning and more application of pacing techniques to all your daily activities. To begin with you might need to tailor your entire day to the programme. In time, you will progress from recovery to 'maintenance' – effectively the same regime as for prevention. This could be a goal over a period of some months. Many sufferers will re-design their regimes at different phases of their condition.

For all regimes you will also need a 'first aid' plan for flare-ups and setbacks. A way to develop this is suggested in Chapter 8.

Whether you go for prevention or recovery management, bear in mind your own capacity for 'keeping at it' over a considerable stretch of time. If you get into the cycle of crisis → action → improvement → inaction → crisis, the period of improvement will be protracted because the body and mind re-learning process at its heart will itself be interrupted.

Facing up to change

Everyone feels resistance to the idea of introducing change into their lives. What they know, what they do, what they may always have done, is safe. It has worked well for them – or well enough – up to now.

If RSI has intervened to make it not work, then it is natural to think of the RSI itself as the unwelcome change which must be driven out so that you can go back to 'normal'. Almost everyone initially focuses on finding the agent – medical or technological – to do this for them.

This is not a sensible approach to your condition. Without your own co-operation – your own willingness to change – there is little likelihood of success. However normal 'normal' seemed, there must be things about how you were functioning in your working and domestic life before the RSI struck you down which were actually not working well for you at all. As you develop a management regime, you will find it easier to identify what these malfunctioning behaviours were and are.

'My body was sending me messages: this situation was no good for me. I was hanging on to it by my fingernails, I was chained to the machine, it felt safe. And it was the opposite of safe. My hands, arms and fingers were telling me I had to let go. Since then, I have entirely changed my approach to life.' *Ken, database administrator*

There is no escape from the reality that developing and carrying out a management regime for your condition will require lifestyle changes. Not only will you need to find time-slots within the day to carry out certain activities – stretches, exercises, relaxation – but you will need to examine your whole way of life, especially your working habits and attitudes.

If you are in a job, this is going to be difficult. Some people are so scared they will lose their job if they admit to having RSI that they do everything they can to avoid telling their employer – including continuing to overuse and overstrain their upper limbs without major adjustment until they are in a far worse condition than they need ever have been.

If you manage to make adjustments, you may improve things to such an extent that you can keep your condition 'under wraps'. But it is far better to address the problem with your employer at an early stage so that work-station changes can be made, and your timetable and the content of your job be made more body-friendly.

> 'I was very reluctant to tell my employer. I thought that there would be a degree of stigma attached to having RSI. So I took annual leave and went to see a physiotherapist. When I went back, I used to do my stretches every hour religiously, but I did them locked in the men's room because I didn't want people to see.' *Jim, software technician*

For many RSI sufferers, the long-term changes required may well mean changing either your job or your occupation or the way you work. Since the last is the easiest change to make, this is where to start. *If you can manage this successfully, you may retain both your job and your occupation.*

Long, intensive periods of keyboarding *must* be broken up. Every 20 minutes, you should get up from your computer, move about, do some stretches (see Chapter 7) and generally get your body moving. If you can do certain tasks without keyboard inputting, take the alternative route.

Analyse all the things you do in which your arms, hands, neck and shoulders are involved. Can you do them in any way which puts them under less pressure? Opening and closing doors for example: can you use your body weight to push open heavy doors instead of your arms? When you're on the phone, are your shoulders or neck in a rigid position? How about a hands-free telephone? When you're reading, are your head and upper body propped up on your bent arm? Find a way to read which allows your arm and hand muscles to be loose and pressure-free.

Don't be so work-obsessed that you neglect the lunch-hour. Don't sit at your desk with a sandwich while you carry on. Go out for a walk. Better still, if you can fit it in, go for a swim. And if you can't do either of these during the lunch-hour, then try to do some kind of fitness programme after work. Try to realize, and feel, that your body has become cramped, immobile and tense during the day and it needs to be freed from an imaginary straitjacket.

On the non-work side, it may be worth examining your diet. Poor eating habits and too much caffeine may be contributing to your problems. If you smoke, that may well be exacerbating your symptoms. In fact, you should examine all the usual behavioural suspects associated with poor physical condition: sedentary lifestyle, lack of aerobic exercise, over-consumption of alcohol, problems with over-weight, high salt intake, inadequate fluids. Improved well-being, however achieved, is going to loosen RSI's grip on your system. And go to bed early! You need to pamper yourself: strain and pain are extremely tiring.

Above all, try to take a more distant view of your work and be more relaxed about it. If you can't shed the cares of the day when you leave the office, go home, put on some loose-fitting clothing, and use some special relaxation techniques to allow this to happen. If your mind is full of tension, it will be virtually impossible for your body not to be full of tension too. And if your body is relaxed, your mind will probably follow suit.

> 'Long term, the shifting of attitude towards work at all levels is where the most important changes are made. These changes are deep and subtle. Other things – treatments and aids – simply support them. By 'all levels', I mean from the gross – cutting down the amount of time spent at the keyboard – to the fine details – considering just how much pressure you put into each keystroke.'
> *Richard, software developer*

Finally, look into the idea of joining a yoga class, a fitness centre, or taking up dance. Do things that help stretch and mobilize your body, but not strenuously. Get to know your body better. Tune into what it is telling you behind the pain. Then the task of managing your RSI and getting it under control will be infinitely easier. Developing this kind of 'bodily awareness' is not narcissistic or self-indulgent. For someone with a chronic pain condition, it is a necessary strategy for survival and improvement.

The two 'Fs' of pain management – fitness and flexibility – will help you to do this. They are the subject of Chapter 7.

7

Fitness and flexibility

Surely I need to rest?

When RSI sufferers find that aches and pains have become acute, they cross a physical and psychological frontier. Suddenly, they are in a state of collapse, have to take time off work and enlist help at home. Suddenly, they are 'ill'.

And what do you do when you are ill? Rest.

Friends, colleagues and medical advisors frequently reinforce the idea that what the body is demanding, above all, is total rest. 'Take some months off' is a common piece of advice. 'Go home and rest, and come and see me when you feel better.'

It seems to make sense. You realize you were putting yourself under great strain. You take to the sofa. Get up late. Watch TV. Read easy pot-boilers. Hand over the household tasks to someone else, or just leave them undone. Give in and *rest, rest, rest*. Until you feel better.

This is not a good idea. In fact, it's a *very bad idea*.

'After my pain got so unbearable that I had to give up work altogether, I spent a lot of time at home resting – getting up late, going to bed early, sitting around. I didn't realize how bad this was for me, how I ought to keep my body moving. Physically, it did me much more harm than good.' *Tracey, researcher*

Obviously, overuse or wrong use of some parts of your body has led to where you are now. That overuse should stop. For a while at least, you will almost certainly need to avoid the activity which caused the problem in the first place – completely. And rest, or rest breaks, must play a part. Structured rest – for example, going to bed earlier or taking a 20-minute nap after lunch to deal with fatigue – is helpful. But complete rest, extended rest, is the last thing your body needs. As little as one week of rest can result in a measurable loss of physical condition – even in fully fit people.

When a person takes bed-rest, the *bones* quickly lose their strength. Every day 3 per cent of calcium is lost; up to 40 per cent in four months. Bones need to bear weight to maintain their strength. Only then does the blood supply flow properly within them and perform its task of nourishing their cells. *Cartilage*, which covers the ends of bones, equally dislikes rest. It receives oxygen and nutrients from lubricating fluid inside the joint which needs to be wiped over all the cartilage and squeezed into it. The cartilage needs a 'drink' of this fluid every few hours. This will happen if the joint is moved around to its full extent in all directions. It will not happen if the body is in constant rest.

Ligaments and *capsules*, which perform critical functions in the working of joints, need to be lubricated too. If they are not stretched gently on a regular basis, they seize up and stiffen. Moving the capsule stimulates its glands to make more fluid, just as we make saliva by chewing on food. Rest reduces lubrication. So, incidentally, does cold – which is why a 'warm-up' is necessary prior to athletic activity.

We all know that *muscles* waste and shrink if we don't use them. On the other hand, if we overuse them they become fatigued. They become tight and fibrous, unable to dispel the toxic residues which build up inside. Soreness, aching and trigger points develop.

RSI sufferers will need to strengthen their muscles on the one hand, and avoid overuse of particular muscles on the other. There is a balance, but rest alone will not achieve it. Rest will make muscles saggy, flabby and unable to support the joints properly. In particular, weakness in the postural muscles – many of which you can feel if you try pulling in your stomach and flattening your lower back against the floor or a chair – will leave your spine inadequately supported. This is potentially disastrous.

Finally, *lungs* and *heart*: sluggish breathing, which dispels only a small proportion of the lung contents, reduces fitness. So does insufficient aerobic exercise: the heart should pump fully for at least a certain amount of time each day. Rest, therefore, has negative effects on these too.

People who suffer from chronic pain typically push themselves until the pain tells them to stop. Then they rest, maybe with a painkiller, and wait for the pain to go away. When they feel better, up they get and try again. This is just the kind of behaviour to expect from driven personalities in an obsessive relationship with their work – as are many computer-pain victims. Soon, the pain recurs. So they stop and rest again. Soon they are locked into a distressing cycle.

The cycle of 'activity → pain → rest' may be repeated daily or over longer periods. Each episode of pain makes it more tempting to avoid activities which lead to pain. Over time, reduced activity leads to unfitness, with joints getting stiffer and muscles weaker. The body cannot cope with much activity at all; less time will be needed to overdo things, and more time dedicated to rest. Eventually, any activity feels like over-activity. RSI is no longer a localized condition, but a general state of system crash.

Your pain has taken control of your life. Your pain is deciding what you do. And you will not be able to recover control until you feel stronger. To get stronger, fitness is an absolute priority. The minute you are fitter, you will almost certainly feel better.

'My body had got into a very sorry state. When your limbs are stiff and unwilling, when you feel pain after a very limited amount of activity, when you feel constantly tired, it's depressing and you feel old. When you start to feel fitter again, it changes your outlook on life entirely.' *Liz, writer*

Introducing exercise into your daily life

However painful your condition, it is essential to introduce regular exercise into your life. Do not succumb to the idea that exercise will cause you further damage and that you must avoid it. This is false.

However, exercise must be done carefully, not stressfully, and not in such a way as to cause a flare-up of pain. If you have become very unfit, your body will probably protest initially – this is unavoidable and you shouldn't be alarmed. You need to start gently and not push yourself too far too fast. This is very important or you will get discouraged and say to yourself: 'This exercise is not for me – I'm not ready for it yet. I'll wait till I'm better.' *Without bodily fitness, you cannot get better.*

To begin with, you may well experience discomfort, shortness of breath, some extra aches and pains. This is normal. Even a top athlete will have these problems after a long break from training. But if you do things gently and increase your level of exercise slowly, you can keep them to a minimum. As you become fitter, they will dwindle away.

If you rush things, or plunge back into a strenuous sport you have temporarily dropped, you will almost certainly give yourself a setback. Pacing – covered in the next chapter – is the key to careful rebuilding of fitness and well-being.

Circuit exercises

This set of exercises (some shown in Figure 3) is designed to cover all needs: weight-bearing for bones, aerobic exercise for heart and lungs, building strength in limbs and muscle groups, especially postural muscles, and stretching to reduce stiffness and elasticize scar tissue.

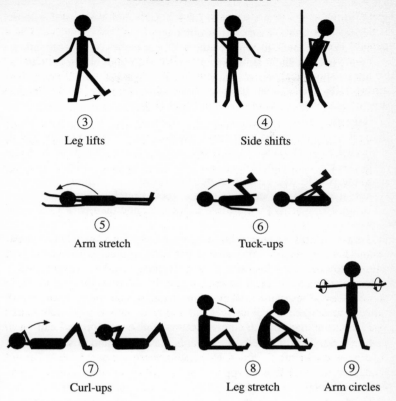

③ Leg lifts

④ Side shifts

⑤ Arm stretch

⑥ Tuck-ups

⑦ Curl-ups

⑧ Leg stretch

⑨ Arm circles

Figure 3. Circuit exercises.

If you choose to adopt this routine, start very modestly, however fit you are. Do no more than a few of any to begin with – the number indicated. If this number seems too many, reduce it. If you have to reduce it to one, try to get through the whole circuit of exercises slowly but surely. If you are already fit, you can add more rounds. If in any doubt, discuss the exercises with a physiotherapist.

1 *Stand-ups*: Sit on a regular upright chair; stand up and sit down. Ten times maximum to begin with.
2 *Chin-ins*: Still sitting on the chair, tuck your chin in, lengthening the back of your neck; hold briefly and release. Repeat five times.
3 *Leg lifts*: Stand, and holding your arms out for balance, lift one leg

up to the side – don't strain or lift too far – and lower to the floor; repeat five times, then do the other leg.

4 *Side shifts*: Stand sideways to the wall, six inches out, feet together. Lean your left shoulder against the wall, with your elbow bent and a little behind you; wrist against your upper waist. Move your hips sideways towards the wall, with knees straight. Then move them out again. This is to loosen your lower back. Do three one side, then three the other.

5 *Arms stretch*: Lie on your back on the floor. Put a thin cushion or a folded blanket under your head if you prefer. Stretch your arms back straight behind your head, keeping your legs straight too. Some people will be able to put their arms on the floor, some will not; it will give your chest area a good stretch either way. Don't strain. Bring arms forward in a half-circle, and then back over your head. Repeat five times.

6 *Tuck-ups*: Still on your back, tuck your knees up towards your chest and hold with your arms around the back of your thighs; lift your nose towards your knees. If they touch, fine, but don't strain. Lower your head and relax, then tuck up again. Five times.

7 *Curl-ups*: These tune your postural muscles. Still lying down, bend your knees keeping your feet flat and your knees hip-width apart. Place your hands with fingers interwoven behind your head as a head-rest. Turn your elbows towards the ceiling and push the small of your back onto the floor. Using your tummy muscles – not lifting your head but merely supporting it – curl up towards your knees. Don't attempt to go too high – just lift your shoulders off the floor. Hold for a breath or two. Then down and fully relax your body. Repeat three times.

8 *Leg stretch*: Sit up on the floor; bend one knee up. Stretch forward with straight arms towards the foot of the straight leg. Hold for a few breaths, then release and reverse the legs, repeating on the other side. Eventually, you may be able to clasp your calf or foot as you stretch forward, but don't push too hard to begin with. Two full rounds.

9 *Arm circles*: Stand and hold your arms out to the side. Make small circles with straight arms and hands. Ten times backwards and ten times forwards.

10 *Stairs*: Walk as briskly as suits you up and down a flight of stairs, of approximately ten treads. No more than two full rounds.

How you do your exercises is very important. For a start, try to overcome the idea that these exercises are a chore. And don't feel that they're an iron-bound regime: introduce minor variations if that suits you. Create circumstances which make their performance easier. Pick a time of day that you can easily make routine. Concentrate on feeling the exercises and the good they are doing your body. If it helps, play music while you do them.

'I feel that even the best physios can be too rigid with their exercise regimes. Much better than doing a fixed number per day is to vary them according to how you are, sometimes more, sometimes less.'
Tim, research historian

It can help to start by giving yourself some encouraging words. Stand tall and spend a minute or so simply tuning in to your body. Take some deep breaths. Then sit down with studied poise. Don't rush through the exercises. Do them *slowly*, smoothly and elegantly. Breathe evenly throughout – and rhythmically with the exercise. For example, when you do chin-ins, breathe in; when you let go, breathe out.

Note which part of the body is being exercised by each particular one. Spine? Back of the legs? Arms? Consciously relax the rest of the body and feel that part alone. If you can begin to identify the parts of your body which are being used in different exercises, you will also be able to tell how they change over time. You may also begin to work out for yourself what postural problems helped bring on your RSI – hunched shoulders? compressed chest? – and therefore what needs special attention. *Bodily awareness is central to managing RSI.*

In the next chapter, techniques for pacing your exercises and building up over time will be described. What it is important to realize at this stage is that exercise, gently done, cannot damage you. So you should establish a routine which is comfortably within your own capacity. If you experience a pain setback worse than just a little extra temporary discomfort, cut back the routine temporarily. You must be able to do it and keep doing it, day in, day out. Once it is well within your capacity, add to it a little. Then stay there for another period of time before increasing again.

'I would start by doing my exercises really thoroughly, and I could feel the difference. But when my condition improved, I lapsed. Then I would get worse, and eventually start exercising again. So I decided the thing to do was allocate 15 minutes every morning; 15 minutes didn't seem so bad. Now I keep it up without an effort. It has become routine.' *Martin, software developer*

It is unnecessary to go on continually adding extra rounds to every exercise over weeks and months. At a certain point decide you have reached maintenance level. It doesn't matter if it is well within your capacity. Take up a sport if you need more exercise than this. *If you make your circuit exercises very long, you will almost certainly get bored and give up doing them.*

Managing your condition requires finding how to initiate and maintain lifestyle changes. Doing what is needed to get fit and stay fit is absolutely critical. So you have to work out how to get yourself to stay with it. Do less than you could, but do it regularly and consistently. Or find someone else to do the exercises with, if that works for you.

There's a good chance you will feel – and look – so much better that you will feel motivated to keep going. But if you find your motivation slipping, take action before pain again overtakes you.

Other paths to fitness

You do not have to be, or to look, sporty to be fit. Different people make different choices for building fitness, and for some, sport is the preferred option. For others, joining an aerobics class, taking up dance or going to a gym may be the answer. Good diet can help build fitness. And there are plenty of everyday ways to take exercise.

'I do a series of stretches and exercises every day, which I regard as very important, and I go swimming once a week. I also bicycle everywhere. I have bought myself an old-fashioned "sit-up-and-beg" bike so there is no pressure on my arms. You can use a very light touch.' *Frances, university lecturer*

Walking

Walking is a very underrated form of exercise, and extremely good for fitness. It has the extra benefit of enabling you to interact with the world, explore the environment, and release stress.

If you are very unfit and walking any distance has become difficult, build up gradually. Think in terms of making small, incremental gains over a long period. For example, if you can only manage a few hundred yards without tiring yourself, just build up to doing those few hundred yards every day to begin with. Then do them two, or three, times a day. If you're fitter and can walk a mile fairly easily, think of doing this on a regular basis. Set targets which work for you: if time is precious, gradually step up your speed, rather than your distance.

How you walk is very important. Incorporate advice on posture into your walking style – or ask a friend to observe you critically. Are you hunching your shoulders against the cold or constantly looking at the ground in front of you? Buy a woolly scarf and stand tall. For carrying things use a small rucksack, not a shoulder bag. Make sure you swing your arms fully – don't carry things under your arm or gripped in your hand. Don't put your hands in your pockets – wear gloves if it's cold. And if you take the dog with you, be careful how you hold the lead. Don't grip constantly, and change it from hand to hand.

For those to whom walking seems too tame, jogging or running may be the answer.

'I bought a pair of running shoes and went out running three or four miles every other day. I swing my arms around a lot, and they do feel a bit sore afterwards, but in the long term it has done me good. It frees me up physically and gets rid of a lot of stress.' *Jim, software technician*

Swimming

Being in the water and swimming around in such a way that your whole body is moving freely has an important effect on symptoms for many RSI sufferers. Those who experience a sense of slow combustion or electrical impulse in the upper body may find that it vanishes after swimming, at least for a while.

'I used to go swimming, for the exercise. Then I had my RSI crisis. One day I realized as I got out of the pool that my symptoms had disappeared – at least at that moment. So then I decided to go swimming every lunchtime, to break the working day. I'm sure it's helped a lot.' *Daisy, writer and editor*

Swimming is also an excellent form of exercise for muscles, heart, lungs. It is also good for releasing stress. But how you go about it is important.

You need to move your limbs extensively in the water to stretch the body. You shouldn't swim with tiny little strokes, nor hold your head rigidly out of the water – this can actually worsen pain in your lower back or stiffen your neck. If you do breast-stroke, buy goggles and put your face in the water. If you already suffer from lower back pain, it may be best to stick to crawl and back-stroke.

Don't thunder up and down but do your strokes smoothly, fully, in an unpressurized way, with maximum extension. Change your strokes – from breast-stroke to back-stroke or crawl after a while – and your movements. Move your focus of attention – from your feet, to your arms, to your neck, to your breathing. Involve yourself in the experience and enjoy the feeling of water around you.

Yoga

Yoga has many forms, but is principally known in its physical form – hatha yoga. However, the word 'yoga' in Sanskrit means union of mind and body, and this ancient science of movement was developed to improve all aspects of life – physical, mental, emotional, spiritual. So although you may decide to try yoga for its physical benefits in helping relieve RSI, you may also find that practising yoga has all sorts of other rehabilitative mental and emotional effects.

Yoga involves practising a series of poses or *asanas*. In many people's minds, yoga poses involve twisting the limbs into all sorts of weird positions: the lotus, with interwoven crossed legs, is often used as the illustrative pose, but there are many others. Don't let this contortionist image of yoga put you off. Some poses are physically undemanding, others can be done in a mild and gentle way. Yoga is not meant to strain your body – everything depends on how the poses are done.

Much of what is involved in yoga – fitness, flexibility, stretching, bodily awareness, breathing deeply, mental and spiritual renewal – is directly in line with the philosophy of pain management advocated for RSI in this book. Therefore, yoga is highly recommended as an antidote to symptoms over the short and long term. There are many books on yoga; consult those at your local library before deciding which to buy. However, it is best to enrol in a class, and use a book as a back-up.

Finding a good yoga teacher is critical. One possibility is to check local classes run by the Community Education Department of your county council. These classes will be run by well-established yoga instructors, which amounts to an endorsement of their quality. They will also probably be subsidized and therefore cost less than those attached to private health clubs or run independently.

If you have done little or no yoga before, go to a beginners' class. Tell the instructor before the first session about your RSI. *Take it easy.* Do not do any pose that you think will cause a flare-up or put your neck, arms, hands, shoulders or other sore area under unnecessary strain. Do everything very gently to begin with. Yoga could be your breakthrough, so don't ruin this possibility by getting with the wrong instructor, in too experienced a class, or overdoing it on the first day.

'I took up yoga after I went on a pain management course. But I did need to achieve a certain level of fitness before I began. I have since found that yoga makes me sleep better, and feel better when I wake up. Just half an hour can make a real difference.' *Liz, writer*

T'ai chi

T'ai chi is another ancient mind–body discipline emanating from Eastern culture. Its purpose is to assist the practitioner to channel his or her energy in such a way as to build harmony within body and mind. It is often described as 'meditation in movement'. It can also be seen as a civilian version of the martial arts, with some affinities to dance therapy.

T'ai chi is based on 'forms', choreographed sets of ritualized movements which restore bodily harmony. In common with postural therapies, the underlying idea is to unlearn set mental and physical patterns with which a person has armoured him- or herself to get through life. The aim is to build up flexibility, suppleness, and sensitivity through controlled but fluid breathing and movement.

T'ai chi can also include exercises, tailored to the individual, which focus on inner strength and balance – for example, by visualizing breath moving through parts of the body. So, like yoga, there are physical and mental ingredients and the level at which a person practices T'ai chi varies. An RSI sufferer might be attracted by the physical side, but come to derive as much from the mental and spiritual.

Other techniques

There are many other mind–body regimes which emphasize fitness and stretching – yoga and T'ai chi are simply the best known and most commonly available. One that may be particularly suited to RSI sufferers is Pilates, described in Chapter 3 under 'Postural retraining techniques' (see page 26). Pilates uses many of the same exercises, or poses, as yoga, and also concentrates on breathing, rhythm, fluency and inner harmony.

'Pilates is excellent for RSI problems – at least I think so and I have tried everything! Whenever I have done too much, I do ten minutes of Pilates and I am fine. So now I have a way of managing my condition.' *Tracey, researcher*

Stretching is vital!

Stretching is just as important as aerobic fitness, in which it plays a part. In fact, it may be more important because as well as keeping muscles and ligaments toned and joints supple, stretching has a role in tissue repair.

After a traumatic injury, such as a flesh wound or fracture, serous fluid is secreted which helps stop any bleeding and begins to glue damaged tissue together. As healing progresses, fibrous tissue – or scar tissue – develops. The fibrous tissue is useful in the early healing process, but it is not as supple and smooth as the tissue it replaces. Like a darned patch, it tends to shorten and tighten the repaired area – in muscle, or in whatever soft tissue has been damaged. So scar tissue needs to be elasticized.

Although there is as yet no proof that RSI involves acute injury to the soft tissue (see Chapter 1), you may find persuasive the idea that stretching tissues is generally useful for healing. One day, perhaps, it will be possible to detect currently invisible scar tissue caused by microscopic injuries to the nerves or nerve sheaths. Whatever turns out to be the definitive cause of RSI-type chronic pain conditions in the upper body, you would be well advised to take stretching seriously.

Almost all RSI sufferers who routinely use stretches as part of their management regime find they make a great deal of difference. Stretching can relieve symptoms immediately; can be used to prevent or postpone the development of symptoms; and can help to relax constantly tensed muscles to permit lasting improvements in your posture.

'The physio I went to inspired confidence. He gave me a lot of stretching exercises to do. He said: "Think about why *you* are getting this, but not others. Your chin is stuck out, your chest is shrunken, your shoulders are rounded, you slouch forward." The exercises aimed to correct much of this.' *Jim, software technician*

Stretches

This set of stretches (some shown in Figure 4) is intended to release tension in your neck and shoulders, stretch your arms and hands, and open up your chest.

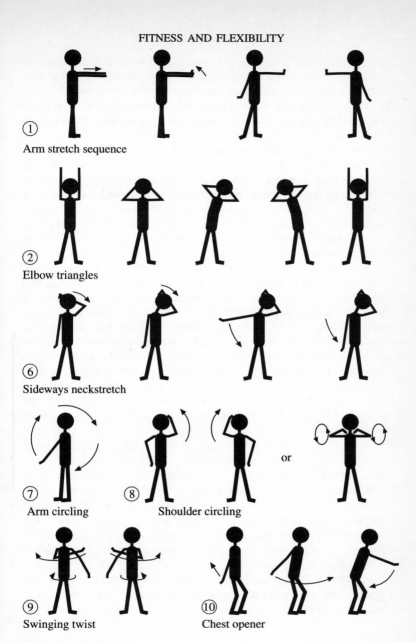

Figure 4. Stretches

83

Bear in mind that all parts of the body are interconnected, and it is beneficial to stretch the whole body. The best thing is to develop your own fuller routine, but these are specially for the upper body.

Most of these stretches are intended to be done standing; some can be done sitting in a chair; a few can be done lying on your back. You may want to ring the changes from time to time.

Before you start, stand tall, breathing easily. Straighten your back and lower your shoulders. Keep your neck long and don't clench your jaw. Every now and again check up on these key areas: *back, neck, shoulders, jaw*, and deliberately loosen them. Remember to work very gently.

1 *Arms stretch sequence*: Raise your arms straight in front of you with palms facing down. Stretch forward as far as you can, pushing your fingertips outwards a little more, on three consecutive outbreaths. Then pull your shoulders back as far as you can, keeping your arms outstretched. Raise your hands from the wrists, so that you have a right angle between hand and forearm. Use one hand to pull the other gently back, retaining the straight arm, on one side and then the other. Then, if you want to, spread the fingers, but not if it is too much for you. Hold for a breath or two keeping elbows straight, then lower hands. Drop arms for a rest if you need one, then raise to the sides. Do the same procedure, stretching out and raising the hand on one side and then the other. Lower arms and rest. Finally, turn the hands front to back a few times, swivelling your arms.

2 *Elbow triangles*: Stretch both arms straight up above head as far as you can, palms facing each other, and look up. Then lower shoulders and look straight ahead. Bend elbows and clasp your hands behind your head. Open up your elbows wide, but try to avoid pushing your head forward. Stay straight and relaxed as you can for a few breaths. Then stretch your arms up again, look up, and lower to your sides. A variation is to bend sideways facing front, first to the right, then to the left, while your hands are clasped behind your head.

3 *Nodding dog*: Make very small up-and-down movements with your nose, meanwhile gradually turning your head to the right. Follow your gaze around as far as you can comfortably go, nodding all the time. Then return, still nodding, and repeat to the other side. Repeat each side, and you will almost certainly find you can see much further round on the second occasion. There are many extra ways to

lubricate the join between neck and head, by nose circling, nodding gently from side to side, nodding while gradually looking up and nodding while looking down. You can also do these movements lightly clasping the back of your neck as if you were holding a dog or cat by the scruff of its neck.

4 *Shoulder stretch*: Clasp your hands behind your back with straight arms. Squeeze your shoulder blades together while pushing your clasped hands away from you and arching your back. Keep your head straight and soft. Relax on the out-breath. Increase the stretch by turning first to one side and holding in that position for a breath or two, then to the other. Breathe evenly.

5 *Up-and-down neck stretch*: Hunch your shoulders, lifting them up to your ears, while breathing in. Breathe out and release. Pull your shoulders down and lift your ears as high as possible, breathing in. Breathe out and release. Repeat a few times.

6 *Sideways neck stretch*: Stretch your right arm up, bend it over your head and hold your left ear. Pull your head gently over to the right, feeling a strong stretch on the left side of your neck. Keep your shoulders down. Breathe evenly for a few breaths and release. A variation is to stretch the other arm out to the side, and gradually lower it, keeping the hand extended while the neck is being stretched. Repeat on the other side.

7 *Arm circling*: Stand with your feet hip-width apart. Slowly circle your right arm in a big arc, letting your eyes follow the finger-tips right round the circle. Breathe in as the arm goes up, breathe out as it goes down. After a few rounds, reverse the direction. Repeat with your left arm.

8 *Shoulder circling*: Keeping your arms loose and hands relaxed, describe a large backward circle with first one elbow, then the other, as if you were doing back-stroke but without straightening your arms. Then repeat going forward, as if doing crawl with bent arms. An alternative version is to put your hands on your shoulders and circle both arms forwards, then backwards.

9 *Swinging twist*: Put your right hand on your left shoulder, then swing your body with your arm fully extended around to the right as far as you can comfortably go, following up with your left hand landing on your right shoulder. Swing round repeating this movement from side to side several times, following the movements of your hands with your eyes. When you finish, you can open up your shoulders by using the free arm to pull the one on the shoulder forward from behind the elbow.

10 *Chest opener*: Stand with legs hip-width apart and knees slightly bent, in a ski-ing position. Fling your arms backward as far up as they will easily go, then let them come forward but not higher than your shoulders; then fling them back again. Repeat many times – say, 20, sometimes with hands facing palms up, sometimes with palms down. Do this quite fast and keep breathing as suits you.

This selection of stretches for the upper body is far from exhaustive. There are many poses and other stretches which can help relax the shoulders, neck and arm muscles or open up the chest. These include the yoga poses known as the 'dog' and 'cat'; the triangle; the bridge; the 'head of cow' and 'eagle' poses; floor twists, forward bends, and many others. However, it is best to learn these under instruction from a qualified yoga teacher.

It is a good idea every now and again to do your stretches and exercises in front of a mirror. You will be amazed to discover that your arm is bent when you thought it was straight, your hand claw-like instead of relaxed, and your head poking forward instead of long and swan-like.

You should always do the stretches in a way that treats your body as a friend. This daily occasion is a tryst you keep with your physical self, for mutual reinforcement. If you do the stretches *slowly*, *smoothly and gracefully*, this will help you to feel good about yourself. Smile a little while you do them.

When you have tried out these stretches, you will probably begin to recognize which ones are especially appropriate for you. Then you can develop your own programme, with variations. You may want to repeat some stretches throughout the day, at your desk, over the stove, in your breaks. For this, pacing is important. That is the subject of Chapter 8.

8

Pain management techniques: pacing

If I do anything for any length of time, it hurts

People suffering from chronic pain conditions naturally shy away from doing the things which bring on their pain. For those with computer-related RSI, this initially means the keyboard or mouse, but it may quickly extend to other activities: writing, chopping vegetables, playing a musical instrument, carrying shopping bags, driving the car.

A common tendency among people suffering from chronic pain is to get into an 'activity → pain → rest' cycle. They push themselves until the pain tells them to stop, then rest up with painkillers until they feel better, then become active again until pain makes them stop once more.

This pattern soon takes on a downwards trend. As the body loses condition, less time is needed to overdo things. Rest or low activity periods become longer, and total daily activity declines. Inactivity thus leads to increased pain – and this, in turn, to despair.

Often, people in this pattern reach the point where they find that if they do anything for any length of time, it hurts.

> 'Physically, rest did me more harm than good. After a while I couldn't even read, write, or watch TV without hurting. And psychologically it was disastrous. I felt I wasn't participating in the world any more. I lost confidence in my ability to be a useful human being, and my social life become non-existent.' *Tracey, researcher*

The consequences of the 'activity → pain → rest' cycle therefore have other dimensions than the physical loss of fitness examined in Chapter 7. They also lead to negative and distressing feelings, to be explored in Chapter 9. People whose pain is not acute, but who are beginning to find that it is insidiously gaining hold over parts of their life – disrupting their working hours or forcing them to drop sports or hobbies – need to consider whether they are not already precipitating the growing command of this cycle over their lives.

Breaking the cycle is difficult. Even those who really want to do so find it hard. It seems as though, whenever they try to do things differently, the pain gets in the way. Or work claims or family responsibilities make them feel they have no choice but to 'soldier on', no matter how severe the consequences.

Some people are so disempowered by their pain that they let it interfere in their judgement. They stay in a job where they are obliged to go on using equipment which is triggering their condition. Many chronic pain victims don't realize they have handed over total control of their life to their pain, letting it dictate when they get up, what they do, whether they can accomplish a task or feel good about themselves in any way.

Do you recognize this behavioural pattern? Have you allowed yourself to let RSI pain symptoms begin to dictate your working, domestic and/or social life? If so, you need to enlist the technique of pacing to re-shape your behaviour and break the cycle.

What is pacing?

As a concept, pacing is familiar. We all know the old adage 'more haste, less speed' and the fable about the race between the sprinting –resting hare and the consistently plodding, ultimately victorious tortoise. At school our teachers repeatedly told us that we would accomplish more by spreading effort over time.

Although we recognize the wisdom of these time-honoured homilies, some of us still persist in exhausting ourselves by up-to-the-deadline concentrated attack, claiming this suits our personalities or work methods best. Perhaps. But it doesn't suit our bodies. Especially when it happens not just every now and again, but over long periods.

Pacing has two forms.

Pacing is, first, a strategic way of slowing down. For those people who conduct their lives on the sprinting–resting pattern, or – worse – the sprinting-only pattern, pacing means a different outlook on life. It requires a more planned, even, measured pattern of activity over the course of the day, the week and the year, and – probably – a calmer, less intense, less impulsive mind-set to go with it. For many people, this involves major lifestyle – and attitudinal – changes. These may seem difficult to begin with, and they do take time.

Pacing is, second, a specific technique, to be applied systematically to all the activities you have given up or reduced as as result of RSI. By applying this technique, you can begin to do them again, and very gradually build up the amount you do them, experiencing much less pain than before. Applying this technique to your daily activities will also, over the longer term, help you abandon a sprinting–resting pattern of life – if that is part of your underlying problem.

Thus in both its general and specific forms, pacing allows you to break the activity → pain → rest cycle.

By using pacing as a systematic technique, *you* – not your pain – are going to prescribe how long you do a certain activity, even if you have to do it initially for a very short time – two minutes, five minutes – to keep it within an acceptable pain threshold.

You are going to alternate essential activities: standing, walking, and sitting. Also specific activities: keying, reading, writing. You are going to match their durations to suit your mental and bodily requirements, balancing 'uptimes' of activity with 'downtimes' of rest and rehabilitation.

'After I'd had serious symptoms for some time, I began to notice that they came on in circumstances far away from the keyboard. Cooking, for example, especially with guests expected. I realized I must pace things better and slow ... everything ... down ...'
Daisy, writer and editor

Example

To give you an illustration on the domestic front. Suppose that you are going to cook a meal. As an experiment in pacing, double the preparation and cooking time. Use the extra time to spread the tasks and take short breaks. Plan ahead the use of all the time, with margins so that you don't have to rush or get tense at any stage. It might go like this:

Setting out utensils, measuring ingredients 10 minutes (walking, reaching and standing).
Break for 10 minutes (sitting or lying down on sofa or floor).
Chopping and peeling ingredients 10 minutes (standing or sitting); if you have to do all this by hand (ask for a food-processor for Christmas!) and it's not finished, have a
Break for 10 minutes, and then complete the task but never chop or peel for more than 10 minutes at a time.
Break for 10 minutes, preferably an active break: walk, do stretches.
Begin the cooking no longer than 10 minutes (probably standing); turn off the gas if necessary and
Break for 10 minutes (sitting/lying down).
Continue cooking no longer than 10 minutes.
Break for 10 minutes.
Etc.

If you tried this and found that it was manageable, next time or the time after you might try increasing the 'uptime' periods to 12 minutes.

You would not alter the length of the 'downtime' until you were really confident. The aim of pacing is to find what you can comfortably manage, work at that level so you become used to it, and then slowly build it up so that the body hardly notices.

Example

Now let us look at an example on the work front: writing a letter on the computer. Note that good planning allows to you minimize actual time at the keyboard.

Planning what you are going to say 15 minutes, lying on your back on the floor or well-supported in a comfortable chair. With arms and body in a relaxed position, just *think*, don't write or make notes.

Break for 10 minutes; make cup of coffee, make phone calls, walk about.

Jot down notes continue thinking if you need to. Up to 15 minutes.

Break for 10 minutes, include movement or stretching.

Keyboard work 5 or 10 minutes depending on your 'tolerance' (see below).

Break for 10 minutes.

Keyboard work 5 or 10 minutes.

Break.

Etc.

If you've become really phobic about keyboards – as some RSI sufferers do – you might need to take this activity a lot more slowly. Or better still, start with other activities to set your pacing.

The five keys to pacing

The five keys to pacing are as follows:

- *Planning ahead*: You must take time to plan ahead. This may be an unfamiliar discipline for those who prefer to be spontaneous. Overcome your resistance and begin to build forward planning into the way you live.
- *Keep a Pain Management Diary*: Pacing requires that you record your day-to-day plans and what you managed to achieve. Use an A4-sized ring-folder so that you can insert pages. Every evening, review what you have achieved; then make a plan for the next day (see below). The diary will enable you to see whether you are making progress and adjust your activities accordingly, instead of stopping an activity only when the pain tells you to.

'Every evening when I went to bed, I would write in my diary "right shoulder, 4, decreasing" or "right arm, 7, increasing", like the weather forecast. I found it reassuring to discover that – contrary to my perception that I was always in pain and it was always getting worse – it went up and down quite a lot.' *Daisy, writer and editor*

- *Take frequent, short breaks*: Whatever the activity, do not go on and on at it. Make yourself stop frequently, and take rest breaks or do other things which are different, physically and mentally. Do not work continuously at the computer for more than 20 minutes.
- *Gradually increase the amount you do*: To start with, you may feel frustrated because you spend so much time planning and taking breaks that everything takes much longer and little seems to get done. But with practice, pacing can become second nature. As the pain is kept at bay, then you can gradually increase 'uptimes' and reduce 'downtimes'. However, *increases and reductions must be very, very gradual.*
- *Break up tasks into smaller pieces*: See any whole task as a series of smaller, contributing tasks. Do each smaller task separately. Take half an hour's gardening, for example. It can be divided up into many activities: weeding, digging, raking, cutting, mowing, etc., some of which require bending, some reaching, some kneeling. Plan the whole task in small pieces, alternating different types of activity.

Putting pacing into practice: establishing baselines

Systematic pacing requires that you establish your body's baseline 'tolerances' for activities which lead to pain. The purpose is to work out how much of an activity you can manage reliably – on both good and bad days. This requires timing.

As an essential first step, get yourself a timer. Even if your watch has one, it is probably better to use a timer which you can put somewhere else, so that you have to get up and walk across the room to turn it off. Get one with a repeat function so that you can set it for – say – 10 minutes, and repeat this 10 minutes again and again.

Example

Establishing your baseline tolerance for keyboard work. Take up your position at the keyboard, and start typing. Go on until you start to feel 'that's enough'. Don't overdo it. Don't be so frightened of pain that you stop too early. And don't push yourself beyond a sensible threshold. Note precisely the length of time you managed – even if it's very short. Don't register a period longer than 20 minutes. Repeat this procedure twice more, at intervals of several hours. Average out the results, and this is your absolute baseline tolerance.

Let us suppose the result was 10 minutes.

Reduce your absolute baseline by 20 per cent or around one-fifth. In this case, to 8 minutes. This is the baseline tolerance you are going to use as a starting point. This means that for the time being, you should not work at the keyboard for more than 8 minutes. To begin with, do this no more than twice or three times a day.

After a week, review your pacing. If you feel that you are gaining in confidence and comfort, you may want to add one minute. This means that you'll work at the keyboard for 9 minutes three times a day the following week; or maybe build to four times a day. See Figure 5 for an example.

For all your activities, review your pacing on a weekly basis (or slightly more often if you are starting from a very low base). Is your level of activity still about right? Too low? Too high? Make the necessary adjustments and re-set the pacing for the following week. But do not become over-confident and increase your times by leaps and jumps. Always build very slowly and by small increments, otherwise you risk a setback. If you are in any doubt, do not make any change.

To start with, you may need to use pacing for all your activities. In each case, start by working out your baseline tolerance, as above. Consider pacing for the following:

- *Essential activities*: activities which have to be undertaken in the course of doing anything else, notably standing, sitting, walking; carrying, holding or lifting things.
- *Domestic activities*: chopping, stirring, hoovering, cleaning, driving, holding phone, book or newspaper, ironing, sewing, DIY, gardening.
- *Work activities*: writing, working at the computer, especially keying in data or word-processing, drawing, designing, reading at your desk.

	Monday	Tuesday	Wednesday	Thursday	Friday	Saturday	Sunday
7–8 a.m.	circuit exercises	same	same	same			
8–9 a.m.	rest breakfast	same	as	same			
9–10 a.m.	stretches rest	shopping	Mon-	stretches rest			
10–11 a.m.	work with	rest stretches	day	trip to			
11–12 noon	breaks	work		London			
12 noon– 1 p.m.	walk						
1–2 p.m.	lunch rest	same					
2–3 p.m.	work with	walk					
3–4 p.m.	breaks	work					
4–5 p.m.	rest relaxation						
5–6 p.m.	work	relaxation rest		relaxation rest			
6–7 p.m.	rest	yoga class		writing w breaks			
7–8 p.m.	supper	supper		supper			
8–9 p.m.	watch tv	read		rest relaxation			
9–10 p.m.	brief relaxation	relax & bed		bed			
10–11 p.m.	& bed						

Figure 5. Weekly timetable

Using pacing in your daily life

Your baseline tolerances are building blocks for the development of a daily pacing plan. Every day – ideally in the evening – sit down with your Pain Management Diary and plan your activities. If you are suffering from a flare-up of pain symptoms, you will need a detailed, hour-by-hour timetable. But routine planning need not be this minute.

Build in plenty of breaks; alternate different kinds of activity and the

93

postures in which they are done; and don't leave out your exercises and stretches. Every day, before you draw up the next plan, reflect carefully on how things went, whether you stuck to the plan, whether it was 'too light', 'about right' or 'too strenuous'. Make adjustments for the next day.

For many people, the most difficult part of pacing is to design the plan in such a way that it is realistic – that conditions exist for you to carry it out and that you do in fact carry it out. Suddenly, you may discover at 10 a.m. that a long phone call or some other unexpected event has thrown you off, and you tell yourself, 'Oh well, it doesn't matter, forget it, I'll have another go tomorrow.' And then tomorrow, somehow, the same thing happens.

For others, the most difficult part is less the need to adjust for unexpected events than to gain the necessary control over the timetable in the first place. You may be running a busy household, having to take children to school and fit in a number of tasks and activities. A serious commitment to pacing all of this seems hopelessly impractical. Or you may be employed in the kind of job or setting where your working day is not at your command, but at the command of your employer, or governed by the nature of the job.

The first thing you have to do is communicate your needs to your family, your partner, your employer, and anyone else whose co-operation you need. (See RSI, Your Employer and the Law (page 119) for guidelines on enlisting the support of your employer.) Explain that your pain condition means that you are going to have to slow down and do less – at least for a while. And explain about pacing, and that you need to stick to a carefully planned timetable. Both at home and at work, try to negotiate your 'uptimes' and 'downtimes' so that they are as convenient as possible both for you and for others.

This course of action is common sense. It is not whingeing, giving-in behaviour. *You have a right to take action to protect your health and your body*. If you don't do so, things will get much worse. If your employer is totally unwilling to co-operate in letting you pace your work, you may need to obtain medical support for time off. As a last resort, leave.

The first rule of pacing while at the computer is that *no bout of computer work should last more than 20 minutes*. You should then break your concentration for at least two minutes of stretches and relaxation. This remains the case if you are using voice recognition software. It is still static, seated work; it can be accompanied by bodily tension; and it can also put a strain on your voice.

If you are the kind of person who persistently forgets or ignores restrictions of this kind, then install a programme on your computer which alerts you to your own time-lines, or forces you to stop for a minute or two by refusing you access to your work at set intervals. (See Useful Resources for suppliers, page 124). If you are able to be disciplined, use a timer. But set it up in such a way that you have to get up from your desk to turn it off.

Intersperse keyboard work with other types of activity. Do all the things that can be done with physical movement in that way, not in a static position. Go out for tea or coffee or use making it to move about. Use phone calls and other opportunities to slow yourself down.

> 'Some of my colleagues would rather send an e-mail to someone just down the passage than get up from their desk and go and speak to them. Apart from being bad for you, it's so impersonal. Whenever I can, I go and speak to people. It provides me with a real change of pace.' *Rosemary, university researcher*

As the days and weeks go by, signs of progress will build your confidence, as pacing allows you to gradually build your activity levels. Psychologically, this is very important. Once you have begun to believe that you are going to be able to increase your level of activity at home or at work, set yourself some long-term goals. Such targets are really important. They can help you both to motivate and to encourage yourself towards recovering your full function.

Perhaps you want to be able to type 500 words without stopping. Work out how many words your current tolerance permits, and decide on a realistic date to target for this achievement. Perhaps you want to cook a recipe you have been avoiding. Again, work out a realistic time-frame for being able to build up your kitchen activity to the point where you could do the work involved without a major problem. When you have achieved these goals, set some new ones.

All small successes build towards a larger success. Along the way, constantly reward small successes. Don't fall into the trap of belittling them because they are so small. If you keep your Pain Management Diary regularly and you read the back entries, you will be surprised to discover what progress you have made.

Putting pacing into practice: exercise

Pacing should be applied consistently to your circuit exercise regime (see Chapter 7). As already explained, if you are very unfit when you start to introduce exercise into your daily life, it is very important to start modestly. If you overdo things, you will stir up your pain.

Apply the same pacing principles to exercise as to other activities. Work out first of all how many of each circuit exercise you should regard as your baseline. Deduct one or two rounds. Then draw up a blank exercise plan to use for the week. Xerox or print out several copies and keep them ready for use in your Pain Management Diary.

Fill in a week ahead the number of times you are going to do each of the exercises. Don't add more than one extra round every three days. And don't go on ever upwards, adding and adding.

If you manage to reach your goal for the week, give yourself a reward.

Pacing does not apply in the same way to stretching. If you choose to have a major stretching session every day, there is no need to increase it unless you want to. The key thing about stretching is that you do it. Any pacing plan should include periods of stretching – short or long – throughout the day.

What do I do if I have a flare-up or setback?

The first thing to realize about flare-ups and setbacks is that *everybody has them*. There are bound to be good days and bad days, days on which you feel things are generally improving and days on which they seem to be getting worse.

Coping with a setback or flare-up requires a special effort at mental fortitude. This is especially true if you have a tendency to catastrophize – to say to yourself: 'Oh my goodness, this is the end, pain management doesn't work for me, I must abandon it,' or words to similar effect. If you carry on like this, you will set yourself up for a long period of trouble. If, on the other hand, you tell yourself that setbacks are normal and can be managed, the pain is likely to retreat more quickly.

The key to managing setbacks and flare-ups is to plan ahead. The earlier you put your plan into action, the more effective it will be. Try to work out what is causing the setback. You may have been overdoing it at the keyboard. Or maybe you have been skimping on stretches or exercises, and it's what you're *not* doing that matters. If you have had a sudden jarring accident – tripped up, for example – this could be to blame. Or if you have been overdoing things generally and become exhausted, this could have activated what has become your 'weak spot'.

First Aid Plan

Have a First Aid Plan ready for home or office, and if you have a bad patch, *use it*. Your First Aid Plan for the office might go like this:

1 Simply *accept* the fact that you're having a bad day; *replan* the next hour – 5 minutes.
2 *Leave your desk* and go for a 10-minute walk, preferably outside in the fresh air. Concentrate on relaxed walking and deep breathing.
3 *Back at your desk*, do some phoning or tidying up – unstressful tasks in which you can move about or at least change position – 20 minutes.
4 *Stretches and sitting exercises* to lengthen neck, stretch arms, open up fingers, etc. – 5 minutes.
5 *Return to work* at the computer using voice recognition software if you have it; if not, do two 5-minute stretches of typing/keying with a 5-minute break between – 15 minutes.
6 *Relaxation break* – 5 minutes.

When the hour is over, reassess your situation. If you are better, step up activity in the next hour, but only very, very slightly. If you feel you have made no improvement, repeat the plan, but extend the breaks.

If things are still getting worse, consider taking some hours off. *But don't give up and go to bed.* Go for a walk, go swimming or give yourself something to boost your spirits – a hot, relaxing bath, for example. Don't stop pacing, or give up your exercises at this point. Take more rest breaks and relaxation.

It can be useful to massage trigger points or sore muscles with your thumb, finger or elbow. An ice pack can also be helpful. If so, have one ready in the freezer, wrap it in a towel and apply it to the most painful area. Don't use it for more than 10 minutes at a time or it may cause a burn.

Back-up plan

If your setback continues for several days, and your First Aid Plan is not really helping, you may decide to take more drastic action. Whatever you do, don't panic. This will just increase your stress level and make things worse. Proceed as follows:

1 Cut down all *tolerances* by half.
2 Cut down all *exercises* by half.

3 Cut down all *activities* by a third or a half, either in terms of how long you are doing them or in terms of how often you are doing them.
4 Develop a plan for getting back to where you were before the setback *within one week*. Build in many relaxations, rest breaks and reinforcers (see next chapter).
5 Give yourself *credit* for how you are coping. Reinforce a positive attitude and try to prevent negative thoughts from taking over.
6 Try to *avoid taking painkillers*. If you do take them, go by the clock and not by the pain.
7 Try to *plan and pace* your daily activities so that *you* are still in charge, not the pain.

If your setback continues for more than a week, re-assess your lifestyle, daily activities, state of mind, and all the things which might be contributing to your condition. Have you been driving too much without taking regular breaks and stretches? Have you been sitting too long in the same position? Has your posture slumped? Are you tense and wound up? Have you been doing too much of something unfamiliar – playing the piano, gardening, painting, or moving furniture around?

'Before, I didn't know how to undertake exercise. Pain came on so quickly whenever I exerted myself that I didn't dare do anything. The scope of my activity and my life became terribly limited. Pacing and building things up gradually was very important for me.' *Liz, writer*

Sticking with it

Applied as a technique, starting from baseline tolerances and building up slowly and systematically, pacing is a way of enabling you to improve your capacity to perform activities you have come to associate with pain. But don't forget that pacing is also an attitude to life and to work. Remember the hare and the tortoise.

If you are the hare type – as many RSI sufferers are – you may quickly find that when your pain condition improves, you abandon tortoise-like behaviour. That behaviour, you say to yourself, was not 'me'. That person who slowed down was the 'me' I want to forget, along with my pain. But if you do this, you will soon be back at square one.

Unless you stick with pacing as a more organized way of life, you are not likely to see any lasting improvement in your RSI condition. Pacing is one of the coping strategies you need to use to be able to be your real self again – however contradictory that sounds.

Pacing means that you need to accept that you will ride through some bad moments of pain and some passages of disappointment. But over time, pacing will allow you to reduce these in both number and duration. The process will be much faster if you can cultivate a favourable mind-set. How to enlist your thoughts and feelings into your pain management regime is the subject of Chapter 9.

9

Pain management techniques: thoughts and feelings

What have my thoughts and feelings got to do with my pain?

If you think that a chronic pain condition such as RSI is purely a physical problem, it's time to think again. What goes on in your heart and mind has a great deal to do with the way you experience your pain and how it affects your behaviour. This is not the same thing as saying that chronic pain conditions exist only in the mind – in fact, it is quite the opposite.

Pain, anxiety, and low mood feed off each other. Anger, depression, and anxiety are known to make pain worse. Pain can also cause a loss of self-confidence and self-esteem. This chapter is about breaking the cycle whereby the pain is bad, therefore your spirits drop; and then the pain gets worse, and so on into a downwards spiral until you can barely distinguish physical from mental agony.

Many people have had an experience with acute injury which shows that the mind can intervene in the experience of pain. Someone injured in a car crash in which others are in desperate need of help may not notice the injury until the others are taken care of, nor feel any pain until that moment of awareness. Similarly, soldiers on a battlefield may manage to carry on until the fighting is over in spite of severe wounds and what ought to be incredible pain.

In the case of chronic pain, where the pain is not unexpected – indeed, may be constantly anticipated – this kind of experience is unlikely. However, many sufferers will have noticed that being distracted can postpone or reduce pain symptoms. For example, an outing to an enjoyable film may turn out fine in spite of prolonged sitting down.

Some people have found that a major change in their emotional circumstances has precipitated improvement. This 'cure' is actually a more positive outlook on life, which made their pain problem seem far less significant, to the point where it ceased to bother them.

'I used to be very driven about work. Now I'm more content, more laid back. I don't work such long hours. Things have changed a lot – partly because I got married in the middle of all these problems, so I'd recommend that!' *Dave, computer programmer*

Some people use preoccupation or 'busyness' as a pain avoidance strategy. But the problem is that if they use it while they are doing something which itself triggers pain – such as working at the keyboard – they will store up worse trouble. However, distraction can be used as a pain management strategy if used positively.

With chronic pain, the body's signalling apparatus via the nervous system has gone awry and 'wrong' pain messages are being delivered to the brain. Stretching, flexibility, and pacing are all strategies for retraining or overriding this dysfunctional circuitry. Working with thoughts and feelings can be seen as a way of enlisting your mental processes to do the same thing. But it is essential to work with *helpful* thoughts and feelings.

Although the mind is capable of banishing or reducing pain symptoms, many people's tendency is to indulge in unhelpful thoughts and feelings which make the pain worse. These thoughts include ideas such as: 'It never stops, it's always getting worse.' Or: 'If this goes on, I shan't be able to work/look after the family/go out tonight/pull my weight in the household,' etc. The sufferer's outlook and behaviour begin to be more closely related to his or her feelings than to the pain.

'The psychological aspect is very important. My life used to be severely limited by my physical condition. I felt very stuck, and that I was likely to get worse. Discovering that I could improve made a huge difference. Feeling that you can improve is half the battle.' *Liz, writer*

When you suffer from chronic pain, especially in the early stages, you may find the mind engaged on the pain all the time: 'Is it better? Worse? In a different place?' This body-monitoring is bound to happen to some extent – and it can be utilized to inform your pacing strategy (see Chapter 8). But if it is entirely fearful and anxiety-ridden, you may come to live your pain to the point where you can't see beyond it. This is unhelpful. This, you have to try and stop.

Coping strategies: interrupting unhelpful thoughts

For some people, even the idea of examining their own thoughts and feelings – let alone trying to do things to change them – is off-putting. You may feel that you already spend enough time thinking about your pain, and the last thing you want to do is analyse the thoughts and feelings associated with it. What you need – you feel – is not analysis, but relief.

The problem is that when you don't get the pain relief you seek – by taking painkillers, for example – you may build up such a level of rage and misery that when you do finally take action, dealing with these emotions will require as much healing as your RSI. Your rage may be directed against an employer, a medical advisor, or perhaps against your partner or yourself. Whoever it is aimed at, it is very little use – and may even make things worse.

> 'I was very angry that this happened to me. I was disgusted with the way [my employer] treated me. It took a huge amount of inner healing to get over it all. I used *Reiki*. I found it very helpful. It got rid of the hurt so I could move forward.' *Pat, computer till store assistant*

Before you can begin to interrupt unhelpful thoughts and feelings you first need to recognize that this is what is going on. A very good way of doing this is to label them by putting them into words. The next time you notice your pain increasing, pick up your Pain Management Diary (see Chapter 8), enter the date and time, and your pain count (on a 0–10 scale). Then make three entries, under: *Situation*, *Thoughts*, and *Feelings*.

Under *Situation*, you might write: 'sending long e-mail'; under *Thoughts*: 'ignored my timer, went on typing too long'; under *Feelings*: 'cross with myself, no self-control'. These thoughts and feelings are frankly unhelpful, and are likely just to make you feel worse, and thereby exacerbate your pain.

Now write two new headings: *Other possible thoughts* and *Other possible feelings*. Spend a few minutes in reflection, and then fill them in. You may want to start with *feelings*. Instead of anger or guilt, why not 'happy at achievement, pleased with myself'? Don't immediately say to yourself, 'How ridiculous!' – just play along with this for a moment.

What *thoughts* might provoke such feelings? How about: 'Managed to complete long e-mail in spite of pain, and resolved to take break earlier next time.' Isn't this more constructive? You might also go out and buy a magazine as a reward for getting the task successfully done.

Next time you notice this 'error' of unhelpful thinking, try to intercept your thoughts and feelings early. You are trying to break your old, self-destructive thought patterns. It may seem odd to begin with, and it is not easy. But it can be done. And when you do manage it, *reward yourself.*

'To get on top of RSI, you've got to stand outside yourself and look at what you're doing, and advise yourself as if you were your own best friend. Counselling is very helpful, especially when it helps you look at the way negative emotions such as fear and anger are impeding your recovery.' *Wendy, computer input operator*

Let's look at an example on the domestic front. Perhaps the *situation* is 'Cooked two-course meal'. Under *thoughts*, you might enter: 'Chose very complicated recipes and got over-tired'. Under *feelings*, 'Why am I such a fool, tired and frazzled?' This crushing assessment is not going to help, especially if you snap at the family and then burst into tears.

So what other *thoughts* or *feelings* might you aim for instead? Thought: 'Meal took longer to prepare than I expected'. Feeling: 'Meal late but doesn't matter!' And if your family or friends find you cheerful and relaxed – in spite of your pain – they probably won't mind if the meal is half an hour late.

The idea of breaking unhelpful thought patterns is the basis of several psychological therapies. If you feel that you need some type of therapy or counselling to help you get started, ask your GP for a recommendation. Asking for help is not an indication of inadequacy. You need to learn a new skill, so what could be more sensible than doing what amounts to taking some lessons?

Learn to lift your own mood – not depend on external factors, such as an encouraging partner or a happy event or a sudden improvement in your condition to do this for you. *Do it for yourself.* Nobody pretends it is easy. Mental patterning is every bit as hard to undo as physical patterning – with which it is often connected. But you have to have hope and believe that things can improve.

Regard the quest for ways of managing your pain as a journey. Use the hope it offers you constructively. Don't set out on the journey saying to yourself: 'I'll give X (Alexander Technique, pacing, Maltron keyboard, yoga) a try, but I bet it won't work for me because I'm . . .' Try substituting: 'I'll give X a try, and there's a good chance it'll work for me because I'm . . .'

Optimism is your ally, defeatism your enemy. Just for a moment, check your facial expression. Lift the corners of your mouth and *smile.* You'll find that your mood will lift too.

Setting goals – and reaching them

Positive thinking is easier if you set yourself some goals. In Chapter 8, we saw how goal-setting is part of pacing; that setting long-term goals – to walk a mile, type a 500-word letter – helps in building up your tolerances. Goals like these are tangible. But the point of setting them is *to motivate yourself.* Goal-setting is therefore a mind activity.

Every week spend a little time working out your short- and medium-term goals. When preparing your exercise sheets (see Chapter 8) you are already attending to your short-term fitness goals. Extend this discipline to your domestic and working life. Every week, set yourself some other goals to accomplish during that week: fix the bathroom shelf, dig up the front border, clear the desk, update your accounts. Enter these goals in your Pain Management Diary.

The goals you aim for may be in areas that present problems because of your RSI, but they don't have to be. Goal-setting helps give structure to a life which has become unfocused and unsuccessful and is making you feel bad about yourself. Achieving the goals will give you a renewed sense of purpose and provide something to congratulate yourself on each week.

If you don't reach your goals, don't punish yourself with accusations of failure. Look at the goals again. Ask yourself: Were they *realistic*? Were they *achievable*? Try being less ambitious next time.

Goals should also be *manageable*: don't get carried away and set too many. Two or three goals in any week is enough. And set one or two long-term goals, against which shorter-term ones might be benchmarks. For example, long-term goal: join a string quartet. Short-term goal: practise instrument for 10 minutes every day.

Goals should also be *measurable*. Set each goal at a specific level so that you will know whether you reach it: for example, if you are trying to build up your carrying tolerances, set a goal such as: carry 3 kg shopping bags for 3 minutes.

Finally, don't just set goals for the sake of it. Set goals which are *desirable*. You may have to make a great effort to achieve them, so you must want to do so.

Many people who have developed chronic pain in their upper limbs have eventually decided to make major changes in their lives – have even used the condition as the starting-point for a new way of life.

'I decided to take voluntary redundancy from my job. I felt very low and was getting no help at all – except months of antidepressants. So I went on a course to qualify me to teach business students. I hoped this would keep me away from the keyboard. I wanted a complete change.' *Deborah, office administrator*

This idea may be strange to people who simply want to go back to 'what I was like and what I was doing before this dreadful thing happened'. Even if this is the case now, your ideas may change. So one possibility is to learn a new skill or take up a new interest. This may lead you somewhere without committing you to a dramatic life change. And it may be enjoyable, and make you feel better about yourself.

For example, you might want to do some kind of voluntary work for a few hours a week. You might learn a new language, or take up painting or photography – something artistic. Introducing this type of change into your life could be an important goal. But don't forget the criteria: *realistic, achievable, manageable, measurable, desirable.*

And don't forget that whenever you achieve what you set out to do, you deserve self-congratulation. Give yourself a reward or reinforcer. Don't move your own goal-posts and say, 'Well, doing that was nothing, after all.' That isn't true from where you were before – as your Pain Management Diary will remind you.

Coping strategies: relaxation and meditation

Relaxation is a vital part of your pain management regime. Being able to relax your body – release your muscles and calm your mind – helps promote well-being generally. It can also help to reduce pain symptoms and tackle underlying problems such as constantly tensed muscles and postural rigidity.

Techniques for relaxation are included in the teaching of yoga and T'ai chi. Meditation, which is usually practised as a means of bringing the mind into a calm, conscious state able to resist bombardment by stressful thoughts, is a parallel technique. Relaxation is a physical state of being, requiring the co-operation of the mind. Meditation can be described as a technique for clearing the mind, requiring the co-operation of the body. They often use the same body–mind routines.

Since relaxation seems to be about doing nothing, people who are driven, workaholic types may have more difficulty with this than with the other ingredients of pain management. However, don't be tempted to skip it. And relaxation does not just mean flopping in a chair to watch television. *You need full bodily and mental relaxation.* If you've never done this properly, maybe it's time to learn.

'I'm an anxious type – that's my personality. I have had a lot of counselling during the past several years. This has had a major effect on my condition, and has enabled me to relax my muscles. Without that, nothing else would have had any effect. A prerequisite for getting over RSI is to be able to relax. One must be able to experience quiet and calm in life.' *Dave, computer programmer*

Anyone with RSI symptoms would do well to join a yoga or T'ai chi class. Meditation can help, too. But once-a-week relaxation is not enough. If you are suffering consistently from pain, at the very minimum you should do two 20-minute periods of relaxation every day. Shorter relaxation breaks should also be built into your pacing and first aid plans. Even if you are only suffering minor pain symptoms, you should still practise some relaxation every day.

Relaxation positions

When setting out to relax your body, it is best to adopt a special position on your back on the floor. The two best positions are known in yoga as the 'semi-supine' position, with knees bent and hands on abdomen; and the supine or 'corpse' position, with arms and legs flat on the floor. A third alternative is to lie with your lower legs and feet on a chair, knees bent at a right angle. Rest your head on a book, folded rug or cushion if you find it more comfortable.

Even if you just adopt one of these positions for 10 minutes, this will help you to relax. Concentrate on letting everything go, breathing deeply and easily, perhaps while playing soothing music. However, if you can learn a technique and use it, this will be much more beneficial.

Once you have learnt how it feels to be relaxed, you can adapt these techniques to use in mini-relaxations when you are sitting at your desk or in a chair, even standing and walking.

For the following techniques, try them out, and if one particularly appeals, try dictating its instructions into a tape recorder. Then you can do the technique without having to read this book at the same time. You can also buy relaxation tapes (see Useful Resources, page 128).

Relaxation technique 1

Lie down in the 'corpse' position. Take a deep in-breath, hold for a moment, and then let the breath out slowly. When the lungs are empty, pause and let the new in-breath enter. Expand your lungs and abdominal area with the new breath. Pause, and then breathe out, releasing your bodily tension with the out-breath. Do a few more breaths like this, observing the breaths travelling through your body.

This kind of slow, deep breathing automatically calms you down. *Do not strain.*

Now take your concentration to your left foot. Tense the foot on the in-breath, and then release all the tension in it on the out-breath. Then move your focus to your left calf. Tense on the in-breath, release on the out-breath. Then to your left thigh; tense and release. Left buttock, tense, release. Continue up your left side: hip area, abdomen, chest, shoulder, arm, hand and fingers, neck, jaw and mouth, nostril, cheek and eye, skull.

Whatever body part you are tensing, be sure to *tense that part only*, keeping all else relaxed.

When you have reached the top of your head, observe your whole body and see if the left side feels different from the right. Then repeat the process going down your right side: head, face, etc., until you reach your right foot. Then observe your body again.

The whole procedure should take several minutes. You can then go round again. Or you can do something slightly different: starting at the left foot and using an imaginary coloured thread, connect all the parts up the left side and down the right. This time, do not do the tense/release action, but simply dwell mentally on each body part, making sure it is relaxed.

This technique not only helps you relax, but helps you learn how to tune in to the different parts of your body – an important skill for managing any pain condition.

Relaxation technique 2

With this technique, lie in the semi-supine position or with your feet on a chair. Repeat the 'breathe in and out' procedure described in technique 1 until your body is relaxed. If you have a tendency to hold tension in some particular part – jaw? neck? lower back? – make a conscious effort to release this area.

Now use your powers of imagination to visualize a peaceful, happy scene. This could be a place you visited on holiday, or as a child, with happy associations. Visit every part of the scene, looking at it from different vantage points – from the sky, from the ground, from different compass points, indoors, outdoors. Imagine a sequence of doing things in the scene. If it is the beach, you could walk along the shore, pick up some shells, paddle in the waves, change into a swimsuit, go swimming, etc.

Another alternative is to imagine yourself in a house you know and like, and walk down a passage and open a door into your own private room. This is a room you have furnished especially for relaxing in and where you feel no pain. Enter the room and enjoy all its features – the colour of its walls, its comfortable chair, its lovely view, the ornaments on the mantelpiece, the log fire. Imagine yourself settling down, listening to music, watching the sunset, or whatever most appeals.

If you find your mind wandering away from the scene, gently bring it back, but do not nag at yourself if this happens. It will probably do so a great deal in the beginning. In time, you will become more practised.

After 20 minutes, bring yourself back to the present. Do a few deep breaths, and gradually wake up your body.

Relaxation technique 3

Take up any of the three positions on your back, and carry out the breathing and relaxing procedure as preparation.

Instead of focusing on a picture, this technique focuses on words. This is similar to the use of a 'mantra'. You can repeat one word, or a sequence of words. One possibility is to count slowly to ten. And then repeat. Do this in time with your breathing.

If you want to use an actual mantra, here is a useful one. It is primarily in word pairs, intended to be internally spoken with the in- and out-breaths. Breathe deeply and pause in between breaths, saying: 'In, out; Deep, slow; Calm, ease; Smile, release; Present moment; wonderful moment'. Take one completely still, silent breath, and then start again. This is a good mantra to use if you can't sleep.

Using any relaxation technique requires setting aside a special time and place each day. However, you can give yourself mini-relaxations throughout the day, wherever you are. At your desk, in the kitchen, in a meeting, walking along the road, driving your car: check for tension in your body, release it, and do some slow breathing or say a mantra to yourself.

If there are situations which you know cause you tension – waiting at the supermarket check-out, queuing at traffic lights, getting instructions from your boss – use these to practise relaxation. Tune in to different parts of your body in sequence, breathe deeply and relax them one by one.

Using relaxation to help you sleep

Many people with pain conditions have a hard time with sleep. And if you don't get enough good sleep, you will feel tired and your pain will likely be worse. Tiredness also exacerbates anxiety or depression. Pain itself is tiring, so when you have a bad day you are likely to need extra sleep. If you have a sleeping problem it is important to address it.

Don't depend on a chemical solution. Using sleeping pills only tends to work for a short while. They are also addictive, so that when you stop taking them, they can lead to a period of anxiety and more sleeplessness.

Try to sort out insomnia by managing your day-time activities and night-time resting pattern better. For example, increase your level of activity during the day and avoid day-time sleep. Don't consume any stimulant – coffee, tea, chocolate, cigarettes – within several hours of bed-time. Don't use alcohol to make you sleep: it may send you off, but makes you wakeful later.

Some people misguidedly think that the minute they lie down in bed, they must by definition be relaxing their bodies. In fact, it is quite possible to be lying in bed comfortably, and still be hanging on like a limpet to bodily stress. The habitual tensions are no more naturally shed than anxieties flooding through your mind – with which they may well be connected.

Test yourself next time you are lying in bed. Is your head drawn into your shoulders, or is your neck relaxed and long? Is your head sinking fully into the pillow? Is your throat clenched? Are your arms or wrists bent awkwardly? Unscrambling all of this is important before settling down for the night, especially if pain is likely to interrupt your sleep.

When you get into bed, put yourself in the semi-supine position, and do a few minutes' deep in- and out-breaths. If you like to read before you go to sleep, it may be a good idea to prop up your head with an extra pillow and read in the semi-supine position. Remove the extra pillow before settling down.

Some people find an orthopaedic pillow with a ridge at the front helps to support the neck and release pressure in the neck/shoulder/throat area. Consult a physio or chiropractor.

The corpse position is more relaxed, but many people prefer to sleep on their side. If you sleep on your side but wake up during the night and cannot get back to sleep, try shifting to the corpse position for a while. Recite a mantra or use another relaxation technique. And remember to be gentle with yourself – you are doing all you can to get better.

Getting the support you need

One of the difficulties facing people with RSI is that others cannot see any evidence of their condition. If your arm was broken, instant sympathy and help would be forthcoming. But a pain condition that is invisible may fail to inspire sympathy – may even be regarded with scepticism.

'My two-year-old loved being swung around, but I didn't dare do it any more because of the pull on my wrists. My family could not understand it. I tried to explain, but it caused quite a lot of aggro. They accused me of making excuses.' *Ken, database administrator*

Another problem with RSI is that, unlike a fracture, the condition is not going to mend any time soon. Some friends or colleagues may avoid asking 'How is your pain condition?' because they don't want to hear the probable answer – that it's not much better. They have nothing to offer so they avoid the subject. This can be hurtful.

Or they may respond in ways that irritate because they're ignorant – like 'Why don't you have an operation?' You may find you don't want to make the effort to explain, so you avoid the subject too. This may make you feel very isolated, a state of mind which can only increase a sense of helplessness.

Try to find ways of explaining your condition, and use them only when you need to – when telling a friend you haven't seen for a while, or when asking for help with carrying things, for example. It's important to communicate the essentials about your condition to those who need to know – family, close friends, colleagues, doctors, therapists, employers; it's also important not to lose valued relationships because you let talking about your pain dominate your interactions.

People may react poorly because they don't understand what it's like to have a chronic pain condition and they don't know how to help. You may experience this as uncaring, but it's a good idea to ask yourself before you start an explanation: 'What do I expect from this person as a result of telling them this? Sympathy? Advice? A new piece of office equipment? Help with the shopping? An evening out to cheer me up?' Let them know what it is you expect, and then at least they can be helpful if they want to.

Many people join RSI support groups. A list of such groups can be provided by the RSI Association (see Useful Resources, page 128). These groups are mostly about exchanging experiences. RSI sufferers can share problems and listen to others, and generally help each other through a difficult time. It is often a great relief to sufferers to find out that they are not alone, and many members of support groups derive a great deal of comfort and useful information from them.

Another useful support mechanism is the RSI-UK e-mail list. RSI sufferers exchange problems, ideas and information via e-mail messages circulated to all members. A website address for the list is given at the end of the book (see Useful Resources).

'I started an RSI support group around 18 months ago because I needed support and I was not getting it. The group is very important to me because these are the only people who really understand what this condition is all about.' *Peter, bank manager*

In the end, people with RSI have to find how to manage the condition themselves. Developing your own pain management regime, and setting yourself goals to aid your recovery, is something no-one else can do for you. The best support – whether from your partner, family, friends or an RSI support group – is support which will help you formulate such a regime and put it into effect, providing encouragement when you need it.

10

Pain management: you can do it!

Are you willing to take on the task?

Throughout this book, the message has been constantly repeated that the critical agent in your recovery will have to be you – not your doctor, not your therapist, not some magical piece of technological wizardry, nor some pill or injection. If you have not been willing to accept this idea, in whole or in part, you are unlikely to have reached this concluding chapter!

Medical research into RSI continues. There may one day be definitive diagnoses for the diffuse forms of pain and paralysis associated with repetitive movements of the hands which, at present, cannot be adequately explained by medical tests. This kind of diagnostic respectability would lead to better recognition of the condition and better chances of financial compensation for those who suffer from it.

Whether the existence of an accepted diagnostic test for RSI would lead to better treatments and medical 'cures' is another matter altogether. It might well not. And whatever financial support any sufferer receives or does not receive from the state or an employer, what anyone in a debilitating state of pain presumably wants above all else is to get better. Or, if the symptoms are not severe, at the very least not to get worse.

Undoubtedly, people who have endured a chronic pain condition for many years face a more difficult uphill climb than those whose symptoms are more recent. Any patterning that is deeply and longlastingly entrenched – as in a folded garment or piece of paper – is very difficult to undo. And some of the patterning we inflict on our bodies has been learnt over the course of our lifetimes, often in mysterious ways. Unlearning or managing to override such patterning may take a very long time. However, it is our conviction that everyone who decides to adopt the pain management route can improve their condition. Not 'most people'. *Everyone.*

But you have to be willing to take on the task. That is essential. You have to be willing to embrace the idea that *you* are going to manage your pain condition – and by managing it, begin to overcome it. Of course, you will still consult others in a position of knowledge, or with a treatment, a technological device, a skill, or some special support or comfort to offer. But the officer-in-charge of your condition will be you.

Abandoning feelings of dependency and powerlessness is something that many people find extremely difficult. When you are incapacitated and in pain, nothing may be more appealing than the sense that someone else – a doctor, a physio, a faith healer – is going to take charge of your life and make everything all right again. One part of the brain may say: 'Pain management makes perfect sense.' Another part may say: 'It'll never work for me', or 'I'll never manage it. There must be something else I can try first.' Feelings of dependency can even be a comfort: 'I've handed this over to the medical consultant or the lawyer. Now all I have to do is wait.'

Try not to postpone embarking on the pain management route until 'something else' has been tried first. The chances are that you are not going to hear any results for months from a medical referral. And if you go to court, you'll probably have to wait years for any outcome. You are bound to experience frustration and stress while waiting for these procedures to crawl forward – frustration and stress which may worsen your condition. When the result comes, it may be disappointing – and if you have pinned your hopes on it, emotionally devastating.

In the meantime, you will be allowing the faulty circuitry in your system to become ever more behaviourally patterned to believe it is doing an excellent job for you, and making it ever less willing to be disentangled.

You need to put one priority above all others in relation to your RSI. *You need to take charge of your condition*, and decide to manage it in such a way that you get better.

Getting your management regime under way

You do not need to cancel everything you have set in motion and start again from scratch. If you have an appointment with a specialist scheduled, or are halfway through a course of alternative therapy, there is no need to make any abrupt change. Instead, review what you are doing, and consider carefully what good it is doing you.

If you have had RSI symptoms for longer than a few weeks or months, you may well be as knowledgeable about your condition as any 'expert'. On the one hand, that may be a discouraging thought. On the other, you should allow yourself to recognize the value of your own judgement concerning your condition.

'When I went to see the pain specialist at a London clinic – an appointment I'd waited several months for – one of the first things he asked was, "What do you think has gone wrong?" I was very impressed with this realization that I might have a useful insight. But it was also a bit unnerving. He was supposed to be the expert.'
Daisy, writer and editor

Consider objectively whether the therapies, consultations, and aids you are using have a valuable potential role in a pain management regime. Assess them as if you were an advisor to someone else. Check whether you are using them just out of blind desperation, in the hope that something will turn out to be 'the answer'. Don't go on with a treatment or technique you really feel isn't achieving anything. Simply cancel the next appointment. You can always go back at a later stage.

Identify, if you can, the key underlying problems which have led to your pain condition. Not 'the keyboard' or 'the mouse' or 'the assembly line' – the external triggering factors – but the things peculiar to you, and which you can influence, which mean that you are in pain while colleagues doing the same work are not. Posture? Stress? Attitude to work? Poorly set up work station?

'Long term, the most important changes came from shifting my attitude to work. Paradoxically, I can now type faster than I could before RSI. This is the result of learning how much tension I was putting into the act of typing. Being sensitive to early signs of things going wrong is also important – telling myself: "Stop work right now!" ' *Richard, software developer*

If you conclude that one of your main problems is a constant state of physical tension, then you are going to build your pain management regime with releasing that as a priority. If you have bad posture, you may decide that postural retraining is your priority. If a driven working style and obsessiveness about work is the major problem, your priority is going to be pacing. Review your current therapies and aids and see if they match your priorities. Keep those that do and regard them as building blocks within your pain management regime. Consider dropping the rest. You will save yourself time and money.

The next thing to do is to buy a loose-leaf folder and a block of A4 paper, and begin your Pain Management Diary. And buy a timer. Start using your timer every evening when you're sitting in front of the television – or whatever you do when you relax. Set the timer for 20 minutes, repeating. Every time it goes off, get up, stretch and move around. Get yourself familiar with the idea of timing, regular movement, frequent breaks, mini-relaxations, and observing your body.

Unless you are in the midst of a crisis and need to be in First Aid mode, break yourself in gradually. Don't turn your life upside down. You won't be able to maintain your regime. Plan each day ahead. But don't make it so drastically different from what you currently do that you'll never keep it up.

If you're trying to control early symptoms, concentrate to begin with simply on slowing down and reducing any activities that trigger pain. At the same time, introduce exercise, stretches and at least one 10-minute relaxation period a day into your life.

If you can just get this routine going, even if later on you recover completely from your RSI symptoms, you may find it so life-sustaining that you continue to do it anyway.

'If someone told me tomorrow that I'd never have RSI again, I'd still do stretching and exercise every day. You need to if you're doing a sedentary job.' *Jo, graphic designer*

Don't forget the pain management formula:

- Two 'Fs': Fitness and Flexibility
- Two 'Ps': Pacing and Postural retraining
- Two 'Rs': Relaxation and Reinforcement

If you need reminding how these all fit together, re-read Chapter 6. It might be a good idea to write out this list with their definitions, and put it in the first section of your Pain Management Diary. Make regular checks to ensure that you do not leave any of them out in your weekly and daily plans, and in your assessments of your achievements.

It is difficult to emphasize enough the benefit of joining some kind of gentle exercise, stretching or bodily awareness class. No matter what your age or fitness, there are so many different types to choose from, many done by local people in community halls or even their homes, that it is very likely that you'll be able to find something to join near where you live. But if it's really not possible, explore the possibility of video tapes – for yoga, Pilates, T'ai chi, etc. (see Useful Resources, page 128).

What are the real chances of improvement?

Experiences with RSI are almost as varied as the number of people who suffer from the various conditions. It is impossible to say whether you will get completely better to the extent that your symptoms will vanish, never to reappear. They might. The likelihood is, though, that they probably will not. Not absolutely and completely. There will always be a 'weak spot' or some tendency to soreness.

But the pain, and all the negative thoughts and feelings associated with it, can be put roundly on the retreat.

If you put into practice the advice in this book, your condition will undoubtedly improve and your pain will be reduced. 'Pain management' is not a cure. Pain management aims to remove the pain, and the accompanying misery, to a level which you can easily cope with. Your pain may remain somewhere in your life, but it will no longer dominate it. And because it is under control, it will cease to cause you so much distress and fear – and you will therefore feel less pain as a result.

Instead of a downward spiral with pain and low mood feeding off each other, you can instigate an upward spiral with reduced pain and better mood reinforcing each other. It may be slow, but, like the tortoise, sure.

When you reach this much better state of mind and physical condition, you may stop desperately seeking a cure for RSI. You may feel it is better not to spend your time and energy focusing on the past, seeking redress for the bad workplace practices or employer negligence which you may feel are to blame for triggering your condition. You may find that you are more interested in getting on with your life within the – by now, manageable – parameters your condition sets.

If you continue to work at the computer – or to do whatever type of repetitive activity triggered your condition in the first place – you are likely to experience some level of symptoms. Even if you don't, acute bodily or psychological stress can still activate an ingrained 'weak spot' so that your old bad circuitry will kick in and your pain recur. But your pain management regime will mean that you will have made changes in the amount you work, and the way you work. For some people, this challenge is one that they come to enjoy rather than reject.

'The onset of RSI is almost a twisted invitation to become creative in finding new ways of doing things. You can't expect to continue doing the things you've done before, in the way you did them. This may mean changing the equipment you work with, or how you work, or even what work you do in the future. The experience is an opportunity to seek a new way of living.' *Ken, database administrator*

Those people who are dedicated to a particular kind of work or career which, however re-adjusted and re-planned, requires some computer use, may well choose to accept that they will have 'bad days'. Some level of pain symptoms may seem acceptable when compared with a total career change. As 'bad days' become fewer and recovery from them quicker, they may seem a relatively minor price to pay – a nuisance to be dealt with, not an incipient disaster threatening the ruin of one's livelihood.

Some long-term sufferers from computer-related RSI or upper limb disorders decide to become self-employed. Central to their pain management regime is putting themselves in a position where they can dictate their working hours, especially the hours they spend at the keyboard. This often represents a dramatic life change, one which is less stable and not as reliable financially as a steady wage or salary. But the sense of personal freedom can turn out to be more than adequate compensation.

'The pain management idea has completely turned my life around. One outcome was that I decided to become self-employed. This gives me control over my working hours. I don't have to do so much keyboard work and I can simply decide: I won't keyboard today. Also, I had stopped going out and lost all my friends. Now I've got all my social life back, too. My life now is actually much better than it was before.' *Tracey, researcher*

In the end, pain management is not so very different from body–mind management, or even life management. Each of these leads to the other. Strange as it may seem if you are in the thick of a pain crisis, managing to set up your own life in such a way as to cope with your condition and get on top of it is a life-enriching experience.

The fact of having achieved this can give you an altogether more balanced, confident and optimistic outlook, and even give you the courage to embark on projects you might otherwise never have tackled. To move house and live in an entirely new area, for example. Or to set up your own company and operate from home.

Once you begin to glimpse these possibilities, the question of whether you are going to get 'completely better' seems redundant. Your life may be fuller, your body fitter, your spirits calmer, and your outlook more hopeful, than they were before the black cloud of RSI descended. All you have to do is keep things that way.

You can do it! Of course you can.

Appendix 1
RSI, your employer and the law

If you have become disabled by RSI, legislation is on your side in the form of the Disability Discrimination Act (1995), the Health and Safety at Work Act (1974), the Management of Health and Safety at Work Regulations (1992), and the Health and Safety (Display Screen Equipment) Regulations (1992) (see page 120). The first of these essentially says that your employer, provided they employ 16 or more people, cannot by law discriminate against you if you are disabled. Current health and safety regulations say that your employer is jointly responsible with you (the employee) for improving your work situation, and providing whatever equipment you need to keep your job.

If you feel that your work equipment needs changing, or that you are being treated unfairly as a result of having RSI, the first thing to do is take it up with your employer. Arm yourself with knowledge in advance – an information pack from the RSI Association is ideal. Your employer, along with most of the rest of the world, is unlikely to understand RSI, and you will need to educate them. If you have severe RSI, your local Disability Employment Advisor should be able to help with advice on equipment, job rotation and work practices, via the government's Access to Work Scheme (see page 120).

If they are uninformed, an employer's attitude will often be that you should take time off work and come back when you're better. But RSI is not like most other illnesses, and it will not usually respond to this simple strategy. Instead, you are likely to need a gradual approach to rehabilitation, as has been advocated by many physiotherapists for years. This will often need to involve a shift in the type of work you do and a downscaling of your workload, to allow recovery, as well as a period of complete rest from the activity that triggered the problem in the first place. Fear not! Most employers are keen to keep staff who are familiar with their job and whom they've taken the trouble to train.

If your employer is one of the few who are unco-operative or antagonistic, you may need to look elsewhere for help (see Useful Resources for contact phone numbers). If you feel that you're being exposed to risk, or that your employer is not carrying out their legal duties, and you have already tried taking this issue up with them to no effect, you can contact your local authority Environmental Health Department (if you work in an office), or the Health and Safety

Executive (if you work in a factory). Such calls are treated in confidence, and the relevant authority will arrange an assessment of the workplace policies, procedures and premises without identifying you.

Taking legal action against your employer is not recommended. Not because it is not justified – it may well be – but because it is highly likely to impede your recovery. And recovery is more important.

Health and Safety (Display Screen Equipment) Regulations

UK government regulations in force since January 1993 require all employers to ensure the health and safety of employees who use VDU equipment for most or all of the day. Under these regulations employers must do the following.

- Assess all work stations to identify hazards and reduce risks – the major hazards being upper limb disorders, visual problems, fatigue and stress.
- Ensure that work equipment, furniture and environment meet minimum ergonomic requirements:
  - screen – adjustable, image stable and adjustable, non-reflective
  - keyboard – good action, adequate hand/wrist support
  - work surface – adequate size and height
  - document holder and footrest provided as required
  - chair – fully adjustable backrest and seat
  - lighting – appropriate, with no glare or reflections
  - noise – acceptably low level
  - temperature and humidity – maintained at comfortable levels
  - software – suitable for its purpose, easy to use, suitably paced, and giving appropriate feedback (e.g. error messages, on-screen help)
- Ensure that VDU work is interspersed with other types of work or breaks.
- Provide eye and eyesight testing for employees, and contribute towards corrective glasses if required.
- Provide health and safety training to ensure correct posture, use and adjustment of work equipment and furniture.
- Provide individuals with health and safety information relating to their work station, and measures taken to comply with the regulations, as a reminder to reinforce training.

Employment Service Access to Work Scheme

Help for people who are disabled by RSI to continue working is available through the government's Access to Work Scheme. The scheme is administered through a network of Placing, Assessment and Counselling Teams (PACTs) throughout England, Scotland and Wales.

PACT advisory workers, called Disability Employment Advisers (DEAs), are attached to local job centres. These are the people to contact for an assessment of your job and work situation. They will discuss with you and your employer the possibilities of you changing jobs within your present company, and of reconstructing your existing job. For RSI, they would usually then refer you for an ergonomic assessment with a technical consultant or ergonomist.

Access to Work makes grants towards the cost of special equipment. For RSI, this might include an ergonomic chair, special keyboard or desk, VR software and, if necessary, a more powerful computer to run it on.

The scheme will fund 80 per cent of the costs over the first £300 for people already in employment, with the employer expected to pay the remaining 20 per cent. For new employees and those who are self-employed, it may fund the full cost of special equipment, depending on the circumstances.

Appendix 2
Useful Resources

Alternative therapy contacts

Find a practitioner under Clinics in the *Yellow Pages*, or contact the
following central organizations for a list of practitioners in your area.

Acupuncture

British Acupuncture Council
Park House
206 Latimer Road
London W10 6RE
Tel: 0208 964 0222

Alexander Technique

Society of Teachers of the Alexander Technique
20 London House
266 Fulham Road
London SW10 9EL
Tel: 0207 351 0828

Chiropractic

British Chiropractic Association
Blagrave House
17 Blagrave Street
Reading
RG1 1QB
Tel: 0118 950 5950

Feldenkrais

Feldenkrais Guild UK
P.O. Box 370
London N10 3XA
Tel: 07000 785506
E-mail: enquiries@feldenkrais.co.uk

Homeopathy

British Homeopathic Association
27a Devonshire Street
London W1N 1RJ
Tel: 0207 935 2163

Kinesiology

The Kinesiology Federation
P.O. Box 17
Woolmer Green
Knebworth
SG3 6UF
Tel: 01438 817998
E-mail: kinesiology@btinternet.com

Massage

British Massage Therapy Council
17 Rymers Lane
Oxford
OX4 3JU
Tel: 01865 774123

Nutritional therapy

Institute for Optimum Nutrition
13 Blades Court
Deodar Road
London
SW15 2NU
Tel: 0208 877 9993

Osteopathy

The Osteopathic Information Service
Osteopathy House
176 Tower Bridge Road
London
SE1 3LU
Tel: 0207 357 6655

Pilates

Body Control Pilates Association
17 Queensbury Mews West
South Kensington
London
SW7 2DY
Tel: 0207 581 7041

Reflexology

The Association of Reflexologists
27 Old Gloucester Street
London
WC1N 3XX
Tel: 0870 567 3320

Shiatsu

The Shiatsu Society
Barber House
Storeys Bar Road
Fengate
Peterborough
PE1 5YS
Tel: 01733 758341

Equipment suppliers

Ergonomic office equipment

Datasound Ltd

Gates House
111/113 Fortis Green
London
N2 9HR
Tel: 0208 883 6421
Website: http://www.datasound.com

Don Johnston Special Needs Ltd

18 Clarendon Court
Calver Road
Winwick Quay
Warrington
WA2 8QP
Tel: 01925 241642
Website: http://www.donjohnston.com

Inclusive Technology

Saddleworth Business Centre
Delph
Oldham
OL3 5DF

Tel: 01457 819790
Fax: 01457 819799
Website: http://www.inclusive.co.uk (Large suppliers of computer software and hardware for special needs.)

Osmond Group Ltd
136 Stanley Green Road
Poole
BH15 3AH
Tel: 01202 777222
Website: http://www.ergonomics.co.uk (Specialists in ergonomic office equipment for people with upper limb disorders.)

PCD Maltron
15 Orchard Lane,
East Molesey
Surrey
KT8 0BN
Tel: 0208 398 3265
Website: http://www.maltron.com (Suppliers of the Maltron ergonomic keyboard.)

Posturite (UK) Ltd
P.O. Box 468
Hailsham
East Sussex
BN27 4LZ
Tel: 01323 833353
Website: http://www.posturite.co.uk (Large suppliers of ergonomic office equipment.)

Mail order suppliers of computer peripherals

Dixons Express	Tel: 01992 503283	Fax: 01992 503061
Inmac	Tel: 0990 134239	Fax: 0990 134242
Misco	Tel: 01933 400400	Fax: 01933 401520
HCS Global	Tel: 0800 252252	Fax: 0800 125125

Voice recognition software and hardware

Dragon Systems UK Ltd

(For DragonDictate, Dragon Naturally Speaking)
Millbank
Pullar Close
Stoke Road
Bishops Cleeve
Cheltenham
GL52 4RW
Tel: 01242 678575
Website: http://www.dragonsys.com

IBM

(For ViaVoice)
Software Enquiry Desk
Tel: 02392 492249
Website: http://www.ibm.com/viavoice

Lernout & Hauspie

(For Kurzweil Voice and Voice Express)
Contact via website: http://lhs.com

Voiceworks Ltd

(UK distributors for PowerSecretary)
Suite 8C
Accommodation Road
London
NW11 8ED
Tel: 0208 455 4750

And specialist independent re-sellers of speech software, hardware and training:

AllVoice Computing plc

Courtenay Park
Newton Abbott
Devon
TQ12 2HB
Tel: 01626 331133
London tel: 0207 600 6700

Fax: 01626 331150
Website: http://www.allvoice.co.uk

The Speech Centre
PS Training & Consultancy Ltd
Newspaper House
8–16 Great New Street
London
EC4A 3BN
Tel: 0207 583 8016
Fax: 0207 353 5004
Website: http://www.psbc.co.uk

Government support services

- *Employment Service Access to Work Scheme* Via local job centres. (See RSI, Your Employer and the Law, page 119.)
- *Disability employment helpline*   0800 528 0462
- *Benefits agency*   0800 882200
- *Health and Safety Executive InfoLine*   0541 545500

Non-governmental support and advisory services

AbilityNet
P.O. Box 94
Warwick
CV34 5WS
Charity specializing in provision of independent information, advice and support for disabled people on the use of computers and associated technology. Around a quarter of their work is with RSI sufferers. Individual needs assessments, and telephone advice. They also hold regular open days.
Tel: 01926 312847
Fax: 01926 311345
Website: http://www.abilitynet.co.uk

Disability Alliance
Charity specializing in advice on rights and benefits for disabled people.
Tel: 0207 247 8763

Disabled Living Foundation

Charity specializing in advice on aids and equipment for home, driving, etc.
Helpline: 03870 603 9177
Website: http://www.dlf.org.uk

National Federation of Access Centres

Network of twenty-eight computer access centres throughout England, Scotland and Wales, mostly based in further education colleges or universities. Free to attending students, but funded through charges to the public for needs assessment. Provide opportunity for independent evaluation of computer equipment, as no direct links to suppliers. Administrative centre based at University of Plymouth.
Tel: 01752 232278

Radar

Campaigning charity which also offers advice on independent living, civil rights, employment, education, benefits, mobility, leisure.
Tel: 0207 250 3222

RSI Association

380–384 Harrow Road
London
W9 2HU
Tel: 0207 266 2000
Fax: 0207 266 4114
Charity providing help and information for RSI sufferers, plus opportunities for networking via a newsletter, annual conference and list of local support groups.

Trade unions

Often good sources of information and support. Contact your own trade union, or find the appropriate one for you via the TUC.
Tel: 0207 636 4030

Print, audiovisual and electronic media

Books

The Mind Body Workout (with Pilates and the Alexander Technique), Lynne Robinson and Helge Fisher. Macmillan (London and Basingstoke), 1998.

Practical Feldenkrais for Dynamic Health, Steven Shafarman. Thorsons (London), 1998.

Your Guide to the Alexander Technique, John Gray. Victor Gollancz (London), 1990.

Classic Yoga: A new approach to fitness and relaxation, Vimla Lalvani. Hamlyn (London), 1996.

Are You Sitting Comfortably? Andrew Wilson. Optima (London), 1994. (Self-help ergonomics book with many tips and tricks for inexpensive work station adjustments.)

VDUs. An Easy Guide to the Regulations (1994) and *Display Screen Equipment Work* (1992), both published by the Health and Safety Executive, and available from HSE books, P.O. Box 1999, Sudbury, Suffolk CO10 6FS. Tel. 01787 881165.

Managing Pain before It Manages You, Margaret A. Caudill. The Guilford Press (New York, London), 1995.

The Optimum Nutrition Bible, Patrick Holford. Judy Piatkus (Publishers) Ltd (London), 1997.

Repetitive Strain Injury: A Computer User's Guide, Emil Pascarelli and Deborah Quilter. John Wiley & Sons, Inc. (New York), 1994.

And best for medical/technical information:
Work-related Upper Limb Disorders: Recognition and Management, Michael A. Hutson. Butterworth-Heinemann (Oxford), 1997.

Relaxation and guided meditation tapes

There are two types of relaxation tapes: mellow music and spoken relaxation or meditation. Most are made by really small companies, so it is impossible to recommend major suppliers. Your best bet is to take advice from a bookshop – 'alternative' bookshops specializing in mind, body and spiritual titles are good sources. Many will sell tapes via mail order, but ideally you should try them out at the point of purchase to check that they will be suitable. No good, for example, if the speaking voice on a guided meditation grates.

Bookshops selling relaxation tapes include:

The Inner Bookshop
111 Magdalen Road
Oxford
OX4 1RQ
Tel: 01865 245301

Watkins

19 Cecil Court
London
WC2N 4EZ
Tel: 0207 836 2182

Courtyard Books

The Glastonbury Experience
2–4 High Street
Glastonbury
BA6 9DU
Tel: 01458 831800

Videos

Public libraries are a good source of videos on a range of exercise and stretching techniques, including yoga, Pilates, and T'ai chi.

Key website addresses

- *RSI-UK* http://www.demon.co.uk/rsi/
- *The RSI-UK mailing list* – an absolute must for RSI sufferers online. To join, send an e-mail to rsi-uk-admin@loud-n-clear.com with the command join rsi-uk.
- *The Typing Injury FAQ* http://www.tifaq.com/ and it's worth subscribing to the online RSI Network Newsletter, via this site.
- *Paul Marxhausen's RSI Primer*
  http://www.engr.unl.edu/ee/eeshop/rsi.html
- *For office ergonomics*
  http://www.ur-net.com/office-ergo/
- *For VR software users* Computing Out Loud:
  http://www.out-loud.com/ and voice-users' mailing list via http://www.voicerecognition.net/
- *For stretching and flexibility* Physiology of Stretching by Brad Appleton:
  http://www.enteract.com/~bradapp/docs/rec/stretching/stretching_1.html

Index